GREAT
BEERS

GREAT BEERS

700 OF THE BEST FROM AROUND THE WORLD

EDITOR-IN-CHIEF **TIM HAMPSON**

LONDON • NEW YORK
MELBOURNE • MUNICH • DELHI

Project Editor Robert Sharman
Project Art Editor Nihal Yesil
Designer Elma Aquino
Managing Editor Dawn Henderson
Managing Art Editors Christine Keilty, Marianne Markham
US Editors Jenny Siklós, Shannon Beatty
DTP Designers Harish Aggarwal, Pushpak Tyagi
DTP Manager Sunil Sharma
Production Manager, DK India Pankaj Sharma
Editorial Manager, DK India Glenda Fernandes
Senior Jacket Designer Nicola Powling
Senior Production Editor Jennifer Murray
Production Controller Hema Gohil
Creative Technical Support Sonia Charbonnier

Content first published in the United States in 2008
in *The Beer Book*
This edition first published 2010 by
DK Publishing
375 Hudson Street
New York, New York 10014

10 11 12 13   10 9 8 7 6 5 4 3 2 1

176461—08/2010

A catalog record for this book is available from
the Library of Congress

ISBN 978-0-7566-5798-7

DK books are available at special discounts when purchased in
bulk for sales promotions, premiums, fund-raising, or educational
use. For details, contact: DK Publishing Special Markets, 375 Hudson
Street, New York, New York 10014 or SpecialSales@dk.com.

Color reproduction by Colourscan, Singapore
Printed and bound in Singapore by Star Standard

Discover more at
www.dk.com

Contents

Introduction

This book is an adventure—a journey through a fascinating world of flavors, colors, and aromas. These pages constitute a trip around the world in 700 ales, porters, and pilsners, and an introduction to the master brewers behind the world's greatest drink.

These are exciting times for beer lovers. With the US leading the way in terms of innovation, in the last few decades brewers have been pushing at boundaries as never before. From Alaska to the Mexican border, America's craft brewers are brewing darker beers, bitterer beers, and hoppier beers than can be found anywhere else in the world. European beer styles are being taken apart and put back together with barely a nod to tradition. In brewing terms, there are simply no rules anymore.

Meanwhile, the great brewing nations of Europe—Germany, Belgium, the Czech Republic—still stand tall, with glorious tradition standing alongside intriguing innovation. Countries historically associated more with grape than grain are also making great strides—Italy's brewers are among the most experimental and ambitious worldwide, and their efforts have been yielding remarkable results.

The other good news for lovers of great beer is that it has never been easier for drinkers to sample such a wide range of beers from around the world. A trip to your local shop or supermarket will in most cases provide a selection of several of the brews featured in this book. More ambitious readers may be encouraged to travel further to track down exciting tipples and experience the brewing and drinking culture of some of the world's top beer destinations. If this appeals to you, this book introduces tours of Oregon, Brussels, the Cotswolds, Prague, and Bamberg—range of destinations representing the best of the old and new worlds of beer.

This book is intended for people who want to broaden their knowledge of beer and hunt down exciting brews from around the globe. It should encourage you never to ask just for a beer without first considering its style—pilsner or wheat, fruit or an American IPA, Belgian ale or a gueuze? For there can be few better pleasures—when returning home after a long day at work or just sitting in a favorite bar—than the pleasure of a great beer. But which one? The choice is yours—enjoy the experience.

Tim Hampson

Aass Bryggeri

Postboks 1530,
N-3007 Drammen, **NORWAY**
www.aass.no

Norway's oldest brewery dates
back to 1834. Named after Poul
Lauritz Aass (pronounced
"ouse"), it is a family-owned
business run by four generations
since 1860.

BREWING SECRET Aass brews
according to the strict 1516 Bavarian Law
of Purity, drawing its water from
the nearby lake of Glitre.

Aass Bock

DUNKLER BOCK **6.5% ABV**
Smooth and creamy; brewed using
Munich malt and Hallertau hops. Lagered
for at least three months.

Aass Juleøl

DUNKLER BOCK **6.2% ABV**
The most sought-after Christmas beer
in Scandinavia. Thick and malty with
a smooth, rich flavor.

Abbaye des Rocs

37, Chaussée Brunehault, B7387
Montignies-sur-Roc, **BELGIUM**
www.abbaye-des-rocs.com

Jean-Pierre Eloir, a former
exciseman, took up brewing in
1979. The business has since
expanded, with the beers gaining
a good reputation, particularly
abroad, and some are now being
developed with export in mind.

BREWING SECRET Core beers are true
to the spiced and well-bodied Walloon
style; keg beers are often unfiltered.

Blanche des Honnelles
WITBIER 6% ABV
Not your usual wheat beer, this one is
made from malted barley, malted wheat,
and home-malted oats.

Abbaye des Rocs Brune
BELGIAN DARK STRONG ALE 9% ABV
Very spiced and sustaining, with a
nourishing touch. Well-liked in Anglo-
Saxon countries.

Achelse Kluis

De Kluis 1, B3930 Hamont-Achel,
BELGIUM
www.achelsekluis.org

At a time when there were many brewery closures, the Belgian beer world had cause to celebrate in 1998. That was when De Achelse Kluis—a Trappist abbey on the Dutch border—started up brewing again after 84 unproductive years! It is run as a pub-brewery, and draws in many passing walkers and cyclists.

Achel Bruin 8

TRAPPIST BEER 8% ABV

More than the draft beers on tap, this is a classic Trappist brew; heavy, estery, and filling.

Achel Extra Bruin

DARK TRAPPIST 9.5% ABV

The flagship of brewmaster Knops—who refuses to drink anything else—rich and rewarding.

Acorn

Wombwell, Barnsley,
South Yorkshire, S73 8HA
ENGLAND
www.acornbrewery.net

One of the newer microbreweries
in England, Acorn was set up
in 2003 and doubled capacity
in its first four years. It now
produces 40 barrels (6,500 liters)
every week.

BREWING SECRET The yeast strain
from the 1850s Barnsley Brewery has
been reintroduced, coinciding with the
company gathering significant awards.

Barnsley Bitter
BITTER 3.8% ABV
Ripe chestnut in color, with a
rounded, rich flavor that lingers
in the bitter finish.

Barnsley Gold
STRONG BITTER 4.3% ABV
Beautifully golden, with citrus fruit hop
aromas orchestrating the ensemble
through to its dry finish.

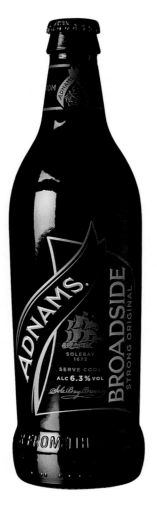

Adnams

Southwold, Suffolk, IP18 6JW
ENGLAND
www.adnams.co.uk

Its "Beers from the Coast" have
been brewed in the classic
English seaside town of
Southwold since 1872. In
recent years, technological
innovation has driven
refurbishment, while an
emphasis on traditional methods
has been studiously maintained.
An eco-friendly distribution
center—complete with living
grass roof—summarizes the
dynamic approach.

Adnams Broadsidee
STRONG BITTER 4.7% ABV
Rich, fruitcake aromas dominate
initially, giving way to an elegant hop
and malt association.

Adnams Bitter
BITTER 3.7% ABV
Aromatic hop and biscuit malt
fragrances introduce a lingering,
dry, and refreshingly bitter flavor.

Airbräu

Münchner Airportcenter,
Terminalstr. Mitte 18, 85356
München, **GERMANY**
www.allresto.de

This brewery has a unique
location: set between the two
terminals of Munich airport.
It opened in 2004 at the same
time as the airport's new
Terminal 2, and it includes a
much-frequented restaurant and
beer garden. Two brewing kettles
are situated right in the middle of
the restaurant.

Fliegerquell
LAGER 5.2% ABV
Deep golden, finely structured,
and classically dry. It is brewed
for international palates.

Kumulus
WHITE BEER 5.4% ABV
Typical yellow color; a sparkling,
very fresh white beer, refreshing
and full-bodied.

Aktien

Hohe Buchleute 3, 87600
Kaufbeuren, **GERMANY**
www.aktienbrauerei.de

The origins of brewing at the
Aktien brewery in Kaufbeuren
can be traced back to the early
14th century. In more recent
times, Aktien has taken over the
Löwen and Rosen breweries.

BREWING SECRET Aktien still brews its
beer strictly according to the Bavarian
Purity Law set in 1516.

Naturtrübes Kellerbier
KELLERBIER 5.1% ABV
Unfiltered and naturally cloudy
out of the cellar. The slightly sweet taste
is typical of one of the oldest styles of beer
in Bavaria.

Fendt Dieselrossöl
MÄRZEN 5.9% ABV
A malty, aromatic structure and
a full-bodied, slightly bitter taste.
Goes well with venison dishes.

Alaskan

5429 Shaune Drive
Juneau, AK 99801, **USA**
www.alaskanbeer.com

Although it is located in a coastal
Alaska community cut off from
the lower 48, Alaskan Brewing
has grown into a force that
spreads from the western coast
of Canada down through much
of the US west of the Rockies.
Founders Geoff and Marcy
Larson focused on native
ingredients and recipes from
the outset. Alaskan's first and
flagship brew, Amber Ale, is
based on a beer made across
the channel from Juneau back
at the turn of the 20th century.

Amber

ALTBIER 5% ABV

Clean caramel on the nose, brightened
by spicy hops. Smooth and malty, with
balanced bitterness.

Barley Wine Ale

BARLEY WINE 10.4% ABV

Cellared in a former gold mine. Rich and
smooth, with dark caramel, cherries, and
plums. Nicely balanced.

A. Le Coq

Tähtvere 56/62,
50050 Tartu, **ESTONIA**
www.alecoq.ee/en

This brewery was founded in
1826, and purchased in 1913
by A. Le Coq, a London-based
company. At the time, it was
looking for a brewery in the
Russian Empire where it could
produce its Imperial Stout rather
than export it from England.
Production was halted in the
1960s but revived in 1999.
A small museum is housed
in the former maltings.

Le Coq Porter
PORTER 6.5% ABV
A strong, dark beer—a worthy
successor to the famous Imperial
Extra Double Stout.

Double Bock
BOCK 8% ABV
A strong and warming light bock,
it has a surprisingly mellow finish
for a beer of this strength.

Alesmith

9368 Cabot Drive
San Diego, CA 92126, **USA**
www.alesmith.com

One of several San Diego
breweries that has pushed
Southern California to the
forefront of national brewing.
It has a wide following for its
mostly strong and often esoteric
beers, many barrel-aged and
vintage-dated.

BREWING SECRET Every employee
is an award-winning home brewer.

Speedway Stout

IMPERIAL STOUT 12% ABV
It's coffee-infused, complementing
a broad imperial palate of chocolate,
toffee, currants, and oily nuts.

IPA

INDIA PALE ALE 7.3% ABV
Brimming with hops and fruit salad
aromas, including notes of ripe mango
and pineapple.

Alhambra

Avenida de Murcia 1,
18012 Granada, **SPAIN**
www.cervezasalhambra.com

The Alhambra group was
founded in 1925 and is named
after Granada's famed Moorish
palace. Spain's purest water
comes from the nearby Sierra
Nevada mountain range, and
is used in the making of
Alhambra beers.

BREWING SECRET The brewery uses
traditional techniques that include
fermentation lasting up to 39 days.

Alhambra Premium
LAGER **4.6%** ABV
A soft gold in color, its nose is lemony
and fresh with a hint of malt. A well-
balanced, quaffable beer.

Mezquita
WHEAT BEER **7.2%** ABV
A full-bodied, assertive red wheat beer
with caramel notes and hints of pepper
in the aroma.

Allagash

100 Industrial Way
Portland, ME 04103, **USA**
www.allagash.com

Focusing on Belgian-inspired
beers, Allagash draws on
tradition but does not shy away
from innovation. In 2007 it
became the first American
brewery to build a traditional
"coolship" (a huge, open,
shallow pan) for spontaneous
fermentation by wild yeasts.

BREWING SECRET Some specialty
beers are aged in oak bourbon barrels.

Allagash White

WITBIER 6.2% ABV
Appropriately cloudy, fruity, and
refreshing. Brightened by subtle
coriander and Curaçao orange peel.

Curieux

TRIPLE 10% ABV
Allagash Tripel ale, aged in Jim Beam
barrels. Orchard fruits and honey meet
bourbon, vanilla, and wood.

Allersheim

Allersheim 6, 37603 Holzminden,
GERMANY
www.brauerei-allersheim.de

Founded in 1854, this brewery
was, for Otto Baumgarten, merely
a sideline to farming. He
harvested the grain in his own
fields, but had to buy in the hops.
Production grew over the years,
though, and today the brewery
has 40 employees.

BREWING SECRET The beers are
brewed to suit discerning local palates.

Landbier
PILSNER 5% ABV
A pilsner with a mash bill from light and
dark malt. Soft in taste, with a typical
malty aroma.

Blue Moon
BEER AND COLA 1.9% ABV
A pleasant mix of dry hops and cola. It's
not too sweet, because the mix is
produced without sugar.

Almond 22

Via Dietro le Mura 36/38,
65010 Spoltore (PE), **ITALY**
www.birraalmond.com

This microbrewery was founded
in 2003, in the seaside town of
Pescara, by Swedish-Italian Jurij
Ferri. He brews highly praised
ales inspired by British and
Belgian styles, as well as some
original, experimental beers that
use local ingredients.

Torbata
BARLEY WINE 8.7% ABV
Peated ale with a smoky flavor similar to a
Scotch whisky. Easy to drink despite its
strength.

Farrotta
SPELT WHEAT ALE 5.7% ABV
Cloudy golden ale brewed using
barley and locally grown spelt; easy-
drinking and thirst-quenching.

Alpirsbach

Alpirsbacher Klosterbräu,
Marktplatz 1, 72275 Alpirsbach,
GERMANY
www.alpirsbacher.de

A railroad was constructed
through the Black Forest at the
end of the 19th century, which
brought many visitors to the
village of Alpirsbach. Johann
Gottfried Glauner helped to cater
for them by reopening the old
village brewery. Sales were good,
and today the beer from
Alpirsbach is produced by the
fourth generation of the family.

Kleiner Mönch

LAGER 5.2% ABV
The golden color promises a fresh, young
beer. It is full-bodied with a flavor of
caramel from the malt.

Schwarzes Pils

PILSNER 4.9% ABV
Deep red-black color and a strong taste,
with a roasted malt aroma that is
unmistakable.

Altöttinger

Altöttinger Hell-Brau,
Herrenmühlstr. 15, 84503 Altötting,
GERMANY
www.altoettinger-hellbraeu.de

The Bavarian town of Altötting is
home to the Altötting Madonna, a
world-famous pilgrimage site. In
1890 Georg Hell expanded
production at a local brewery to
help cater to thirsty pilgrims.
Today the brewery produces
eight different beers.

BREWING SECRET The finest hops and
best German malts are used.

Bayerische Dunkel
DUNKEL 5.2% ABV
Roasty and malty taste, but fresh, and
with a long finish. A dark specialty with
its own character.

Fein-Herb
LAGER 5% ABV
The best malts, combined with a
careful selection of hops, produce
an exceptionally dry, fine taste.

Amber

Bielkówko, ul. Gregorkiewicza 1,
83-050 Kolbud, **POLAND**
www.browar-amber.pl

Owned by the Przybylo family,
this medium-sized brewery is one
of the most modern in Poland.
Situated close to Gdansk in
Pomerania, an area with a rich
brewing tradition, the brewery
is a supporter of the Slow Food
movement, and organizes the
Kozlaki Bielkowskie food and
drink festival every September.

Koźlak

DUNKEL BOCK **6.5**% ABV

A ruby-red beer, it is rich in malt and
yeasty flavors, with a warming aftertaste.

Zywe

PILSNER **6.2**% ABV

Pale in color, it has lemon flavors
and uses hops and barley from the
Lubin region.

Amsterdam Brewing

21 Bathurst Street, Toronto,
Ontario, M5V 2NG, **CANADA**
www.amsterdambeer.com

Purity, passion, and revelry are
the watchwords for Toronto's first
brewpub. Founded in 1986, it was
an immediate success. Business
was brisk, and it soon moved to
another site before finding its
current home in 2005. The brewery
stands opposite the historic Fort
York, the 1793 birthplace of
modern Toronto. In 2003, when
the Kawartha Lakes Brewing
Company closed, its brands were
sold to Amsterdam Brewing.

KLB Nut Brown Ale

BROWN ALE 5% ABV

The unmistakable tang of East Kent
Golding hops. Sweet to taste, it has hints
of honey and chocolate.

Amsterdam Wheat Beer

WHEAT BEER 4% ABV

Light in color, with malt sweetness and a
hint of fresh bread. Often served chilled
with a slice of lemon.

Anchor

705 Mariposa St.
San Francisco, CA 94107, **USA**
www.anchorbrewing.com

Fritz Maytag saved Anchor
Brewing from closing in 1965,
introduced US drinkers to many
classic styles, and launched a
microbrewery revolution.

BREWING SECRET Maytag is known for
preserving the indigenous "steam style,"
which involves using bottom-fermenting
yeast at high temperatures in wide,
shallow, open pans.

Liberty Ale
PALE ALE **6**% ABV

A benchmark American pale ale. Fruity
and floral on the nose; crisp bitterness on
the palate.

Anchor Steam
STEAM BEER **4.9**% ABV

A signature woody, minty nose. Well-
rounded caramel flavors yield to a firm,
crisp finish.

Andechs

Kloster Andechs, Bergstr. 2,
82346 Andechs, **GERMANY**
www.andechs.de

The Benedictine monks of
Andechs began to produce beer
in 1455. The monastery updated
its brewery in 1972, investing in
modern equipment. Still closely
associated with the holy
mountain pilgrimage site
southwest of Munich, Andechs
today is a brand name that's
internationally known.

Bergbock Hell
BOCK 7% ABV

A strong beer, but it tastes mild and
aromatic. Its typical light sweetness gives
it a full body.

Doppelbock Dunkel
BOCK 7% ABV

This world-famous beer has a really
strong taste. The dark malts give it an
unmistakable character, with a light
aroma of hops in the finish.

Anderson Valley

17700 Highway 253
Boonville, CA 95415, **USA**
www.avbc.com

Set in Mendocino County's picturesque Anderson Valley, this solar-powered brewery mixes local and international styles and techniques. Some beer names are those of local landmarks, others are in Boontling, a regional dialect.

BREWING SECRET The copper brew kettles were rescued from a closed-down German brewery.

Boont ESB
EXTRA SPECIAL BITTER 6.8% ABV
Citrussy hops layer fruit on top of bready malt. Tangy in the middle; a long and mildly bitter finish.

Barney Flats Oatmeal Stout
OATMEAL STOUT 5.7% ABV
Impression of coffee and cream, sweetness balanced by roasted grains, the complexity heightened by earthy undertones.

Anheuser-Busch

One Busch Plaza
St. Louis, MO 63119, **USA**
www.anheuser-busch.com

Anheuser-Busch brews half the
beer sold in the United States,
including Budweiser and Bud
Light, two of the world's best-
selling brands. With its Michelob
line, seasonal specialties,
and beers produced by its
regional breweries for local
consumers, the company has
significantly broadened the
range of its beers.

Michelob

MALT LAGER 5% ABV
Returned to its all-malt roots in 2007.
Delicate, with a spicy nose, clean malt
middle and crisp, dry finish.

Stone Mill Organic Pale Ale

PALE ALE 5.5% ABV
Organic beer under the Green Valley
Brewing label. This ale is lightly bready
with earthy hop character.

Anker

Guido Gezellelaan 49,
B2800 Mechelen, **BELGIUM**
www.hetanker.be

Now here's a brewery with a
history. The owners claim it
began in 1369, but it was in 1873
that the Van Breedam family took
over and began its modern
brewing age. In the 1990s, the
end for the classic Gouden
Carolus seemed near, but a
family buy-out from the ill-fated
RIVA empire succeeded, and now
the brewery is productive and
innovative once more.

Gouden Carolus Classic
STRONG DARK ALE 8.5% ABV
This malt bomb has a characteristic taste
of raisins in portwine. An exemplary
strong, dark Belgian ale.

Gouden Carolus Christmas
STRONG DARK ALE 10.5% ABV
The raisins and molasses from the
Carolus Classic are present, but with a
greater alcohol kick.

Ankerbräu Nordlingen

Ankergasse 4, 86720 Nördlingen,
GERMANY
www.ankerbrauerei.de

The brewery's history can be traced from 1608, when several beers were brewed here for a festival. It was acquired by the Grandel family at the end of the 19th century.

BREWING SECRET The beers are made with local malts, mineral water from the Ries, and hops from Spalt.

Lager Hell
LAGER 5% ABV
A full-flavored clear, yellow beer; pleasant and full-bodied, with a fine aroma at the beginning.

Nördlinger Premium Pils
PILSNER 4.7% ABV
A very flowery hop aroma turns slightly bitter and a bit sparkling on the tongue.

Antares

17 Esquina 71, La Plata - P de Bs As,
7600, **ARGENTINA**
www.cervezaantares.com.ar

Antares is the brightest star
in the Scorpius constellation,
and the brewpub that shares its
name sparkles too. Stylish and
smart, it offers a lively alternative
to beers from international
brewers. Brews include a kölsch,
a Scotch ale, a honey beer, a
cream stout, a barley wine, and
an imperial stout, with some
variations in style.

Antares Stout Imperial

IMPERIAL STOUT 8.5% ABV

Intense liquorice and toasted flavors give
way to roasted coffee and caramelized
orange intensities.

Antares Kölsch

KÖLSCH 5% ABV

A well hopped and highly drinkable ale
style. Good fruity overtones make it an
ideal partner to food.

Apatinska Pivara

Trg Oslobodenja 5, Apatin,
25260 **SERBIA**
www.inbev.com

The biggest brewer in Serbia
and the largest in the Balkans,
this InBev-owned company
now has 46 percent of the local
market. The town of Apatini,
which is on the Danube, is in a
fertile barley-growing area
called Vojvodina. Records show
that brewing has taken place in
the town since 1756.

Jelen Pivo
LAGER 5% ABV
Light yellow in color, with a white,
wispy head. It has hints of grass and
grain and aromas of hops and malt.
Jelen means "deer."

Apatinsko Pivo
LAGER 5% ABV
A fresh-tasting beer with floral notes and
a citrus aroma.

Arcadia

103 West Michigan Avenue
Battle Creek, MI 49017, **USA**
www.arcadiabrewingcompany.com

Using the British Peter Austin
system more common in the
Northeast, and brewing with
British malts, Arcadia leans
toward UK-inspired ales, but
made with citrussy and piney
Pacific Northwest hops.
Ringwood yeast gives the beers a
fresh character, and they work
particularly well on cask.

London Porter
PORTER 7.2% ABV
Rich on the nose, flavors of coffee
beans, chocolate, and dark fruit, with
a lingering, dessertlike finish.

Scotch Ale
SCOTTISH ALE 7.5% ABV
Nuttiness and piney hops don't totally
balance here. The final impression is
of sweet caramel.

Arco

Schlossallee 1, 94554 Moos,
GERMANY
www.arcobraeu.de

Arco has been owned by the
Counts of Arco-Zinneberg for
450 years. The castle and brewery
belonging to the family are
situated in Moos, a small town in
the heart of Niederbayern
in Bavaria, where the rivers Isar
and Donau converge. The current
Count Arco personally launched
the beers in the US in 2004.

Schloss Hell

LAGER 4.9% ABV
With its soft but full-bodied taste and
golden color, Arco's Schloss Hell typifies
Bavarian lager.

Urfass

LAGER 5.2% ABV
Slightly more bitter than the Schloss Hell,
and especially spicy, this is a real
premium lager of Bavaria.

Asia Pacific Breweries

459 Jalan Ahmad Ibrahim,
639934 **SINGAPORE**
www.tigerbeer.com

Widely available across Asia,
AP's beers are now brewed in
seven different countries. Tiger
Beer—its most famous—was first
produced in the 1930s, when the
"Time for a Tiger" slogan was
first used. Anthony Burgess
named the first novel in his The
Long Day Wanes trilogy *Time
for a Tiger*.

Tiger

LAGER 5% ABV

A golden colored refreshing lager. It is
normally served so chilled that its taste
and aromas are masked.

ABC Extra Stout

STOUT 8% ABV

A strong but easy-drinking beer. The nose
is robust, with roasted coffee and
chocolate flavors.

Auer

Münchner Str. 80, 83022 Rosenheim,
GERMANY
www.auerbraeu.de

Between 1887 and 1920, Johann
Auer acquired several plots of
land and some breweries around
the town of Rosenheim,
southeast of Munich. Since
then, the company has
expanded considerably.

BREWING SECRET When it was
founded, this was one of the most
modern breweries in Bavaria.

Bajuware Dunkel
DUNKEL 5.5% ABV
Brewed in old-fashioned Bavarian
style, this beer has a malty aroma
and a full-bodied character.

Weizenbock
WHEAT BOCK 7% ABV
A strong, spicy specialty. A good
accompaniment to hearty cheeses
or sweet desserts.

Augustiner

Landsberger Str. 31-35, 80339
München, **GERMANY**
www.augustiner-braeu.de

Founded in 1328, this is the
oldest brewery in Munich and
one of only two in the city (along
with Hofbräu München) that do
not belong to a giant of the global
brewing industry. The site as it
is today was constructed in 1885.
Augustiner beer has become
famous around the world even
though the brewery does not
advertise itself.

Edelstoff
EXPORT **5.6%** ABV
The unusual dark golden color
displays its special character. A sweet
and obvious hop taste guides you to
a very malty finish.

Weissbier
WHEAT BEER **5.4%** ABV
Golden and cloudy, this is a full-bodied
wheat beer with a citrus taste and light
bitters in the finish.

August Schell

1860 Schell Road
New Ulm, MN 56073, **USA**
www.schellsbrewery.com

Family-owned since August
Schell founded it in 1860, this
brewery has perhaps the most
beautiful setting in the US, with
ornamental gardens and a former
carriage house converted into a
museum. In 2002 the company
took over production of the
legendary Grain Belt Premium
beer, when that brewery failed,
to save a Minnesota icon
from extinction.

Caramel Bock
BOCK **5.6**% ABV
Rich caramel on the nose, turning
rummy on the palate. Sweetness
lingers after a not-quite dry finish.

Schmaltz Alt
ALTBIER **5**% ABV
Subtle combination of biscuit and
chocolate balanced by mild, slightly
spicy hop flavors and bitterness.

Au in der Hallertau

Schlossbrauerei Au in der Hallertau,
Schlossbräugasse 2, 84072 Au,
GERMANY
www.auer-bier.de

Au is at the heart of the largest
hop-growing area in the world.
It was linked with the master
brewer Schweiger in 1590 and,
since 1846, has been owned by
six generations of the Earls
Beck of Peccoz. A modern
approach is an essential feature
of the management at Au in
der Hallertau.

Hopfengold

EXPORT 5% ABV

Golden color, full-bodied taste with fine
bitters of hops and clear malt. Nice finish,
not too sweet.

Holledauer Leichtes

WHEAT BEER 3.3% ABV

A cloudy yellow, light wheat beer, fresh
and lightly sparkling; not too heavy a
taste, and with a slightly bitter finish.

Avery

5763 Arapahoe Avenue
Boulder, CO 80803, **USA**
www.averybrewing.com

Located near the Rocky
Mountains, though in a
nondescript industrial park,
this brewery has earned a
reputation for its hoppy beers
and its astonishingly strong
beers (sometimes they are both).
These include a threesome
nicknamed the "Demons of Ale,"
in which the beers average
15 percent ABV apiece.

India Pale Ale

INDIA PALE ALE **6.3%** ABV
Piney, oily nose, with grapefruit and
orange from the aroma to the palate.
Unapologetically bitter.

Salvation

BELGIAN STRONG GOLDEN ALE **9%** ABV
Fleshy fruits, particularly apricots,
mingle with sweet, spicy aromas and
flavors, and a surprising hint of honey.

Ayinger

Zornedinger Str. 1,
85653 Aying, **GERMANY**
www.ayinger.de

Johann Liebhard founded this
brewery in Aying in 1876, at
a time when there were about
6,000 breweries in Bavaria.
That number has dropped to
about 700 today, but Ayinger
has survived and was renovated
by the Inselkammer family in
1999. It has since become more
widely known.

Jahrhundertbier
EXPORT 5.5% ABV
A honeylike aroma with light flowery
hops leads on to a harmonious finish.

Celebrator
DOPPELBOCK 6.7% ABV
The taste of malt dominates this nearly
black, strong beer. It is not as sweet as
other doppelbocks of the same quality.

Baird Brewing

9-4 Senbonminato-cho, Numazu City,
Shizuoka 410-0845, **JAPAN**
www.bairdbeer.com

Founded by Ohio native Bryan
Baird and his wife Sayuri in
January 2001, Baird has come
to be considered Japan's best
brewery. After the six regular
beers were established—later
augmented by an American-style
wheat ale—Baird then focused on
many seasonal beers. The Bairds
have recently opened a taproom
in Tokyo.

Rising Sun Pale Ale

PALE ALE 5% ABV

A brilliant American-style Pale Ale made
with British Maris Otter malt and with
a unique US hop signature.

Angry Boy Brown Ale

BROWN ALE 6.2% ABV

Exciting and complex, this strong brown
ale has a complex flavor profile and
a richly satisfying finish.

Le Baladin

Piazza V Luglio 15,
12060 Piozzo (CN), **ITALY**
www.birreria.com

Charismatic, pioneering Teo
Musso is internationally
known as one of the most
creative brewers in the world.
He has turned beer into a type of
wine and created beer truffles—
not even he knows what he will
do next.

BREWING SECRET Musso plays music
to his yeasts during the fermentation
process, believing that they respond.

Xyauyù

BARLEY WINE 12% ABV
Radical oxidization gives "solera"
sherrylike favors. A flat, warming,
velvety nightcap. A masterpiece.

Nora

SPICED ALE 6.8% ABV
Inspired by ancient Egypt, using kamut
grains, ginger, and myrrh.
A balsamic bitterness comes from
Ethiopian resins.

Baltika

6 Proezd, Parnas 4,
St. Petersburg, **RUSSIA**
www.eng.baltika.ru

The Russian beer market has been going through a period of rapid change as it continues to adjust to a capitalist economy. Baltika's rise has been swift, and it is now the country's largest beer producer. It brews the top two brands—Baltika and Arsenalnoye. The company accounts for more than seven out of ten beer sales, and exports to 46 countries.

Baltika No.3 Classic

LAGER 4.8% ABV

A malty nose gives way to a bitter finish. Widely available across Russia.

Baltika No.6 Porter

PORTER 7% ABV

A well-balanced beer. Dark roasted malts, chocolate and molasses flavors fill the glass, overlayed by a good hop finish.

Barley

Via C. Colombo, 09040 Maracalagonis
(CA), Sardinia, **ITALY**
www.barley.it

Skilful home brewer Nicola Perra
established this microbrewery in
2006 in southern Sardinia,
challenging the mass-market
lagers so popular in the region
(consumption here is the highest
in Italy).

BREWING SECRET Local ingredients
such as Sardinian wine wort and organic
honey are used in the ales.

Toccadibò
GOLDEN STRONG ALE 8.4% ABV
A warming ale; spicy, hoppy and dry,
with intriguing bitter-almond notes
of amaretto.

BB 10
BARLEY WINE 10% ABV
A unique brew made with *sapa*, the boiled
wort of local Cannonau grapes. A highly
distinctive nightcap.

Barons

1 Moncur Street, Woollahra,
New South Wales 2025, **AUSTRALIA**
www.baronsbrewing.com

"Beer barons" by name and
nature, this relative newcomer
has its brands produced under
contract and is one of the
country's fastest-growing craft
beer players; they are also
eyeing export markets in the
US and Russia.

BREWING SECRET Barons makes use of
indigenous "bush tucker" ingredients,
such as wattle seed and lemon myrtle.

Lemon Myrtle Witbier
BELGIAN WITBIER 5% ABV
Moderate carbonation, lime-scented
mid-palate with spicy hints, followed by a
clean, crisp finish.

Black Wattle Original Ale
SPICED AMBER ALE 5.8% ABV
Creamy mouthfeel, malt-driven, with
hints of roasted nuts, chocolate, and
milky coffee.

Bateman

Wainfleet, Lincolnshire,
PE24 4JE **ENGLAND**
www.bateman.co.uk

One of the country's oldest and
most picturesque family
breweries—with a windmill
towering high above—it has a
well-deserved reputation for
"good honest ales." A family
split almost destroyed the
business in the 1980s, but it
survived, blossomed, and has
developed a new brewhouse and
engaging visitor center.

XXXB

STRONG BITTER **4.8% ABV**
Classic russet-tan ale, with a well
constructed blend of malt, hops,
and fruitiness.

XB Bitter

BITTER **3.7% ABV**
Finely balanced, with an apple-influenced
hop aroma that lingers alongside the
malty flavor.

Bath Ales

Warmley, Bristol,
BS30 8XN **ENGLAND**
www.bathales.com

The founders' brewing
backgrounds and insistence on
traditional methods operating
alongside cutting-edge
technology has resulted in Bath
Ale's reputation for distinctive,
characterful, and flavorsome
ales. The success of the business
has led to the brewery twice
outgrowing its premises since
it was established in 1995. A
bottling plant and shop continue
the growth.

Gem Bitter
BEST BITTER **4.1**% ABV
Rich and full-textured, with a malt, fruit,
and bitter-sweet hop quality throughout.

Special Pale Ale (SPA)
PALE ALE **3.7**% ABV
A prominent hop aroma and bitter
malty touch complement its
light-bodied character.

Bathams

Brierley Hill, West Midlands,
DY5 2TN **ENGLAND**
www.bathams.com

The brewery's frontage—actually
the Vine Inn—is emblazoned
with a quotation from
Shakespeare's *Two Gentlemen of
Verona:* "Blessing of you: You
brew good ale." Five generations
of the Batham family have been
involved since the brewery was
established in 1877, each
nurturing its reputation
for classic Black Country
mild ales.

Bathams Best Bitter
BEST BITTER 4.5% ABV
Straw-colored ale, with an initial
sweetness, soon overtaken by a
complex, dry, hoppy flavor.

Bathams Mild Ale
MILD 3.5% ABV
A fruity, dark brown mild; sweet
and well-balanced, with a hoppy
fruit finish.

Bavik

Rijksweg 33, B-8531 Bavikhove
Harelbeke, **BELGIUM**
www.bavik.be

With the fourth generation of
the De Brabandere family, this
brewery is run efficiently and
encompasses a large number
of tied pubs too.

BREWING SECRET Abbey ales and
pilsners form an important role in
the annual output (especially to
supermarkets), but the most interesting
brews are in the oud bruin tradition.

Petrus Oud Bruin (Dark)
OUD BRUIN **5.5% ABV**
Recently, the brewery invested in giant
wooden barrels for fermenting this
vinous, quite traditional ale.

Petrus Aged Pale
OUD BRUIN **7.3% ABV**
In the new barrels, you'll find this: the
undiluted pale beer, ageing for years,
gaining sourish, fruity notes.

Bayern Meister Bier

1254-1 Kawaharabata,
Inouede-aza, Fujinomiya City,
Shizuoka 418-0103, **JAPAN**
www.bmbier.com

Brewmaster Stefan Rager
originally came to Japan to
brew at several start-up
microbreweries which opened
after the 1995 liberalization.
Later, with his Japanese wife,
he founded a boutique-style
brewery on the southern face
of Mount Fuji, dedicated to
German beer styles. The German
Embassy in Tokyo is one of his
most loyal customers.

Prinz Pils
PILSNER 5.5% ABV
Pale yellow, soft mouthfeel with low
carbonation. The subtle flavors are
in excellent balance.

Amadeus Doppelbock
DOPPELBOCK 8% ABV
Very deep reddish brown, with coffee,
toffee, and caramel aromas. Rich tangy
malt and high alcohol suggest rum-
soaked fruitcake.

Bear Republic

345 Healdsburg Avenue
Healdsburg, CA 95448, **USA**
www.bearrepublic.com

With a brewpub located amidst the Sonoma County wine-tasting rooms and a brewery north of town, Bear Republic presents a decidedly different break for wine tourists. Founding brewmaster (and fireman and race-car-driver) Richard Norgrove is just as skilled as any wine blender when merging hops flavors and aromas.

Racer 5
INDIA PALE ALE 7% ABV
Delightfully fresh grapefruit and thick piney aromas, built on a resinous, malty-sweet middle.

Hop Rod Rye
IMPERIAL INDIA PALE ALE 8% ABV
Bright, citrussy nose with spicy alcohols. A subtle blend of biscuit and clean rye. Incessant hops.

Beba

Viale Italia 11,
10069 Villar Perosa (TO), **ITALY**
www.birrabeba.it

Pioneering brothers Alessandro
and Enrico Borio brew a wide
range of regular and seasonal
lagers at their microbrewery
founded in 1996 near Turin. The
adjoining tap-room serves all the
house beers on draft along with
excellent food. The local specialty
is *gofri*, a crisp unleavened bread
stuffed with cheeses, cured
meats, or preserves.

Motor Oil

STRONG DARK LAGER 8% ABV
Ebony-colored, with strong notes of
liquorice and roasted coffee, beans
and a long, bitter finish. As viscous as
its namesake.

Talco

RYE LAGER 4.2% ABV
Seasonal "rye weizen-lager" is a
thirst-quenching treat on a hot
summer afternoon.

Bell's

8938 Krum Avenue
Galesburg, MI 49053, **USA**
www.bellsbeer.com

The oldest surviving microbrewery east of Colorado, Bell's (formerly Kalamazoo Brewing) has grown nearly 700-fold since its first sales in 1985. Bell's has built a new brewing facility outside Kalamazoo, but the original brewery remains, along with its appropriately named Eccentric Café. Bell's beers are famous for their intensity, although the brewery flagship is wheat-based.

Expedition Stout

IMPERIAL STOUT 11.5% ABV
Begins with an intense blast of dark fruit (figs and plums) that turns into chocolate, roasted coffee, and port.

Oberon Ale

WHEAT BEER 5.8% ABV
A summer refresher. Zesty, with orange rind in the aroma, and delicate spiciness behind that. A crisp, sharp finish.

Bere Romania

Str. Manastur Nr. 2-6,
Cluj Napoca, **ROMANIA**
www.sabmiller.com

Now a subsidiary of SABMiller, this brewery first opened in 1878. Its main brand, Ursus, is advertised under the slogan "The King of Romanian Beers." Each September the town of Cluj Napoca, in the heart of Transylvania, hosts a beer festival.

BREWING SECRET These beers are fermented using Bavarian yeast.

Ursus Premium Pils
PILSNER 5.2% ABV
Lively carbonation, a malty aroma, hints of fresh hops and bread, and lemony notes in the finish.

Timisoreana
LAGER 5% ABV
A light yellow, easy-drinking beer that doesn't challenge the senses. Made to a recipe from 1718.

Berg

Berg Brauerei Ulrich Zimmermann,
Brauhausstr. 2, 89548 Ehingen-Berg,
GERMANY
www.bergbier.de

Berg, founded in 1757, is family-
owned and one of the smallest
breweries in Germany.

BREWING SECRET Berg makes use of
corn in brewing, which is supplied
by an organic farm nearby.

Berg Original
LAGER **4.8**% ABV
Its smooth, dry taste makes this
beer the most popular brand offered
by the brewery.

Berg Märzen
MÄRZEN **6.1**% ABV
A typical strong beer. The taste is very
hearty, not least because of its high dose
of hops.

Bergquell

Weststr. 7, Löbau, **GERMANY**
www.bergquell-loebau.de

With its long brewing tradition, the Bergquell Brauerei Löbau has played an important role in the Lausitz region since 1846. It is also one of the most advanced breweries in the whole of Germany and is well known for its wide range of special beers.

BREWING SECRET The special beers have an international following.

Kirsch Porter
PORTER 4.2% ABV
A black beer with a cherry flavor and typical porter qualities. Malty and full-bodied.

Lausitzer Porter
PORTER 4.4% ABV
Typical porter with a dry, roasted malt taste. It is full-bodied and not too heavy; dark colored and a little bit sweet.

Berkshire

12 Railroad Street South
Deerfield, MA 01373, **USA**
www.berkshirebrewingcompany.com

Western Massachusetts' local
brewery (although its beers are
increasingly easy to find in
Boston). BBC handles almost
all its own distribution,
guaranteeing that its beer will
be fresh and retain a subtle,
balanced complexity that begins
with open fermentation.

BREWING SECRET These pure,
unfiltered beers must be
kept refrigerated.

Drayman's Porter
PORTER 6.2% ABV
Coffeelike aromas, a complex middle
(chocolate and toffee), and a pleasantly
bitter finish.

Raspberry Strong Ale
FRUIT BEER 9% ABV
Brewed with fresh berries and released
for Valentine's Day. Scarily nicknamed
"Truth Serum."

Berliner Kindl-Schultheiss

Indira-Ghandi-Str. 66-69, 13053
Berlin, **GERMANY**
www.berliner-kindl.de

The union of the Berliner Kindl
and Berliner Schultheiss
breweries in 2006 was symbolic
for Germany, whose breweries
had declined through post-War
division. The merger has
generated a great many new
brands, produced in one of the
most modern brewing facilities
in Germany.

Märkischer Landmann
SCHWARZBIER 4.9% ABV
Black and highly malty, but without any
bitterness. A genuine original of the
Märkish region.

Bockbier
BOCK 7% ABV
Golden, strong, and not too sweet;
pleasant, with a smooth finish—
a typical bock.

Bernard

5 Května č.1, 396 01 Humpolec,
CZECH REPUBLIC
www.bernard.cz

While reviving 16th-century
Humpolec brewery in 1991,
Stanislav Bernard and two
partners took the daring
decision to produce traditional
unpasteurized beers using
microfiltration. Since then,
awards and an expanding
export market have followed.

BREWING SECRET Bernard has its own
floor maltings and uses spring water.

Celebration / Sváteční Ležák
PREMIUM LAGER 5% ABV
Delicate herblike hop and yeast
aromas overlay a peppery bitterness
for a grassy finish.

Amber / Jantarový Ležák
AMBER BEER 4.4% ABV
Brewed using caramalt for a nutty
bitterness, offset by toffee aromas
and a honeyed palate.

Big Sky

5417 Trumpeter Way
Missoula, MT 59808, **USA**
www.bigskybrew.com

Three partners successfully
combined a quality ale with a
clever name (albeit one it had to
defend in lawsuits lodged by
Canadian brewer Moosehead)
and an attractive label. Big Sky
has grown quickly into a regional
brewery selling beer from Alaska
to Minnesota, three-quarters of it
their flagship brown ale.

Moose Drool
BROWN ALE 5.3% ABV
Dark fruits and nuts mingle with
chocolate; sweetness moderated by
earthy hop notes. Chocolate-brown with a
medium body.

Scape Goat Pale Ale
PALE ALE 4.7% ABV
Biscuity, fruity, and spicy on the palate,
balanced by moderate bitterness. Short
but dry finish.

Birrificio Italiano

Via Castello 51, 22070 Lurago
Marinon (CO), **ITALY**
www.birrificio.it

Agostino Arioli founded his
renowned brewpub in 1994 with
his brother Stefano and other
friends. His pils and bock soon
became cult favorites. He brews a
large range of seasonal beers
such as a sparkling blackcurrant
lager and a cask-conditioned
ale spiced with cinnamon and
ginger. The restaurant serves
great regional food and has
live music.

Scires
CHERRY ALE 7% ABV
Whole black Vignola cherries, lactic
bacteria, wild yeast, and wood chips
create this fantastic sour beer.

Fleurette
FLAVORED LIGHT ALE 3.7% ABV
Made with barley, wheat, and rye,
and flavored with rose and violet petals,
elderberry juice, black pepper, and
citrus honey.

Bischoff

Wellerhof, 50321 Brühl,
GERMANY
www.bischoff-koelsch.de

This privately owned brewery
was established in farm
buildings at the beginning of the
1960s, in an area of Brühl, near
Cologne, that has been inhabited
since Roman times.

BREWING SECRET The brewery's
kölsch is a specialty of the Cologne
region and is traditionally served in
a tall, narrow glass.

Bischoff Kölsch
KÖLSCH 4.9% ABV
Clear golden color; fresh and sweet, with
light notes of hops.

Radler
BEER BLEND 2.5% ABV
Clear yellow in color, with lemonade-
citrus aromas. It is sparkling and
very refreshing.

Bischofshof

Heitzerstr. 2, 93049 Regensburg,
GERMANY
www.bischofshof.de

The Bischofshof brewery started
life attached to Regensburg
Cathedral. Records show that it
was brewing in 1230 for the
Bishop. At the beginning of the
20th century, it moved to a
new location in order to expand.
Nowadays, Bischofshof beer is
produced in one of the most
modern facilities in the
brewing industry.

Weissbier Hell
WHEAT BEER 5.1% ABV
An old Bavarian specialty: fresh, clear,
sparkling, and slightly sweet—in a
pleasant way.

Bischofshof Pils
PILSNER 5.1% ABV
Creamy foam and a light, sparkling
start. Good bitter taste; light aromas
of fine hops.

Bitburger

Römermauer. 3, 54634 Bitburg/ Eifel,
GERMANY
www.bitburger.de

Founded in 1817, Bitburger is a
pilsner specialist. It is well
known through international
sponsorship of sporting events,
and is widely regarded as the
best brewery for pilsner on draft.

BREWING SECRET The company always
uses two-row summer barley, and its
testing brewery is unique in Germany.

Premium Pils
PILSNER 4.8% ABV
A clear, typical pilsner with a light, bitter
taste; smooth, but very dry. On draft it is
fresh and elegant.

Bitburger Light
PILSNER 2.8% ABV
The light sister of the premium. Though
only 2.8% ABV, it is full-bodied, with a
fresh cask taste.

Black Sheep

Masham, North Yorkshire,
HG4 4EN **ENGLAND**
www.blacksheepbrewery.com

The Theakston family has brewed
in Masham, North Yorkshire, for
six generations, but a loss of
independence led to Paul
Theakston stepping aside. He
then established Black Sheep in
a former maltings sitting high
above the Ure River. Since 1992,
Black Sheep has enjoyed
continuous growth, physically
and in reputation, resulting in a
£5m doubling of capacity in 2006.

Black Sheep Ale
BITTER **4.4%** ABV
Full-flavored, with a rich, fruity aroma,
bitter-sweet malty taste, and long,
dry finish.

Riggwelter
PREMIUM BITTER **5.9%** ABV
A strong, complex, fruity bitter,
with dashes of pear drops and hints
of liquorice.

Blaugies

435, Rue de la Frontière,
B7370 Dour-Blaugies, **BELGIUM**
www.brasseriedeblaugies.com

Hard by the French border,
Blaugies is another small family
brewery in which the children
have taken over from the
parents—who, in this case,
started up the business in 1988.
The aim of De Blaugies is
to produce beers in the style of
the region, and the brewery often
creates highly unusual brews.

La Moneuse

SAISON **8**% ABV

Down-to-earth, spicy Hainaut brew:
yeasty, estery; strong for a *saison*, with
the characteristic metallic tang.

Bière Darbyste

FLAVORED ALE **5.4**% ABV

Fig's juice? Alcoholic variant of
Yesteryear, a non-alcoholic brew. Sweet
only when fresh.

Blonder Sörgyar

Futca 9 Vonyarcvashegy, **HUNGARY**
www.blonder.hu

One of a handful of
microbreweries to have emerged
in recent years in Hungary,
Blonder Sörgyar is situated close
to Lake Balaton, the largest
lake in central Europe. As well as
beer brewed on the premises,
this roadside inn offers
accommodation and has a
restaurant. The food is very
Hungarian—wholesome, and a
fine accompaniment to the beer.

Világos
LAGER 5.6% ABV
Yellow in color, this is a strong, grainy
beer with an overt sweetness. Somewhat
rough at the edges, but it works very well
with Hungarian cuisine.

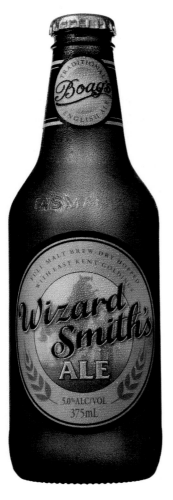

J Boag & Son

39 William Street, Launceston,
Tasmania 7250, **AUSTRALI**a
www.boags.com.au

From a once-moribund regional
brewery, Boag's has ridden a
wave of popularity since the
launch of James Boag's Premium
Lager in 1994. Lagers comprise
the bulk of production, but
Boag's has rolled out some
fine limited-edition ales in
recent years. The brewery was
acquired by the Lion Nathan
group in late 2007.

Wizard Smith's Ale

BITTER ALE 5% ABV
A solid malt backbone, with toffee and
spicy hop notes, is rounded out by a
significant bitterness.

Bockor

Kwabrugstraat 5, B8510 Bellegem,
BELGIUM
www.bockor.be

This brewery is probably best known for its Jacobins (would-be lambics that use spontaneous fermentation). However, the brewery turns out a whole range of other beers, not least a traditional style oud bruin, created by former head brewer Omer Vander Ghinste. Bockor is currently revamping the range of beers.

Bellegems Bruin

MIXED FERMENTATION BEER 5.5% ABV
Oud bruin relies both on wild and cultivated yeasts. The result: a beer in which flavors of berries, wood, and lactic sourness abound.

Bøgedal Bryghus

Høllundvej 9, DK-7100 Vejle,
DENMARK
www.boegedal.com

This farmhouse is the world's only commercial brewery producing the old Danish style of "Goodbeer," a strong, rich beer dating back to before the industrial age. The same recipe is always followed, and yet no two beers are alike, hence they are numbered rather than named.

BREWING SECRET Bøgedal is Scandinavia's only all-gravity brewery.

Brew No. 127

DARK ALE **6.3% ABV**
Smells of prunes and citrus. Fills the palate and lingers on with a faint smoky aftertaste.

Brew No. 121

PALE ALE **5.9% ABV**
Light amber in color with compact carbonation. Aromatic sweetness reaveals notes of honey, citrus, and fine wine.

BØGEDAL Nº 127
Type: Mørk, Northern Brewer, Appelsin
Alkohol: 6,5 %
Brygget: 2/4 2008
Tappet: 15/4 2008

Boon

Fonteinstraat 65,
B1520 Lembeek, **BELGIUM**
www.boon.be

In 1975, when lambic-based beers
and lambic brewers were dying
out, Frank Boon took over the De
Vits range. Deemed crazy, he still
proves his detractors wrong, by
constantly growing and
improving his business.

BREWING SECRET Most Boon beers are
deemed "oude," meaning "in the old
style" of unadulterated lambics.

Geuze Boon Mariage Parfait
GUEUZE 8% ABV
"Perfect marriage," meaning the lambics,
of course, resulting in the brewers'
favorite dry gueuze.

Boon Oude Kriek
KRIEKEN 6.5% ABV
A fully unsweetened krieken (sour
cherry) lambic, which makes this beer
a delight for tongue and eyes.

Boon Rawd

999 Samsen Road, Bangkok,
10300 **THAILAND**
www.boonrawd.co.th

Boon Rawd was founded in 1933
by Phraya Bhirom Bhakdi, who
had toured Germany and
Denmark to learn about brewing.
The brewery is still owned by the
Bhirom-Bhakdi family. The
company operates three
breweries in Thailand.

Singha
LAGER 6% ABV
A full-bodied barley malt beer with a
strong hop character. Clean to taste, it
complements spicy food.

Singha Light
LAGER 3.5% ABV
Lacks the complexity and vitality of its
stronger stablemate. It is pale yellow of
hue and thin to taste.

Boscos

Various locations in Tennessee
and Arkansas, **USA**
www.boscosbeer.com

Since 1992 this brewpub
chain has been a leader in
promoting greater knowledge
of beer in the mid-south. Its
pubs feature English-inspired
cask-conditioned ales, with
customers invited to participate
as cellermen.

BREWING SECRET Flaming Stone's
brewing process involves red-hot chunks
of granite being plunged into the wort to
caramelize the sugars.

Flaming Stone Beer
STEINBEER **4.8%** ABV
Brewed in the manner of German stein
beers. Caramel, toffee, and nuts
throughout. Smoky, dry finish.

Hefeweizen
HEFEWEIZEN **4.8%** ABV
Classic bubblegum and banana nose;
softer fruity (more banana) and creamy
flavors, with underlying spices including
light clove notes.

Bosteels

Kerkstraat 96,
B9255 Buggenhout, **BELGIUM**
www.bestbelgianspecialbeers.be

It is now the seventh generation of the Bosteels family that owns and runs this brewery. In recent times, they have shown a flair for flowing with fashion—not only in the beers, but also with spectacular glassware.

BREWING SECRET Tripel Karmeliet, one of the flagship beers, uses three grains in the mash: barley, wheat, and oats.

Tripel Karmeliet
ABBEY TRIPLE 8% ABV
Smoked and spicy nose announces a malt-dominated brew with a roasted character—unusual for a pale beer.

Deus Brut Des Flandres
BELGIAN STRONG ALE 11.5% ABV
The Dom Perignon lookalike bottle shows that this is aimed at upmarket drinkers; dry and spritzy.

Boulder

2880 Wilderness Place
Boulder, CO 80301, **USA**
www.boulderbeer.com

The first US microbrewery outside of California, Boulder has been something of a poster child for the "movement" because its partners began brewing in a goat shed and it relied on the largesse of domestic giant Coors to acquire ingredients. Boulder Beer is available in much of the US, and emphasizes its Colorado roots.

Planet Porter
PORTER 5.1% ABV
The brewery's original beer. Dark fruit aromas and flavors. Subdued roasted malts and bitterness.

Hazed & Infused
PALE ALE 4.85% ABV
As hazy as promised—hops in suspension—supported by a bouquet of citrus, flowers, and spices.

Bourganel

7 avenue Claude Expilly,
07600 Vals les Bains, **FRANCE**
www.bieres-bourganel.com

In 1997 Christian Bourganel,
a drinks distributor in the
Ardèche, decided to develop a
range of blonde artisan beers
flavored with regional produce.

BREWING SECRET Unusual ingredients
include chestnuts (*marrons*), bilberries
(*myrtilles*), nougat from Montélimar and
Verveine du Velay liqueur, which
is flavored with verbena.

Bourganel au Nougat
FLAVORED LAGER 5% ABV
An amazing nougat bouquet and, in the
mouth, the flavor of grilled almonds.

Bourganel aux Marrons
FLAVORED LAGER 5% ABV
An amber beer; elegant, very fruity and
refreshing, with a hint of vanilla as well
as chestnut.

Brains

Crawshay Street, Cardiff,
Glamorgan, CF10 1SP **WALES**
www.sabrain.com

A major force in regional
brewing, Brains is tremendously
proud of its Welsh heritage. Ales
are produced in a traditional
fashion at the company's
landmark Cardiff Brewery, to
which it was relocated in 2000
from the nearby Old Brewery,
where the famous "pint of
Brains" had been produced for
more than 100 years.

Brains SA Gold
BEST BITTER 4.2% ABV
Its spirit aroma blends gentle malt
and spiced hop with malt-rich and
fruit flavors.

Brains Bitter
BITTER 3.7% ABV
Rich amber color, with subtle malt and
crisp hop aromas. Well balanced, with
some bitterness.

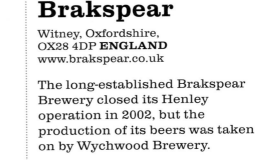

Brakspear

Witney, Oxfordshire,
OX28 4DP **ENGLAND**
www.brakspear.co.uk

The long-established Brakspear
Brewery closed its Henley
operation in 2002, but the
production of its beers was taken
on by Wychwood Brewery.

BREWING SECRET Wychwood uses
Brakspear's original equipment to brew
these beers, including the unique "double
drop" wooden fermenting vessels, and its
complex yeast strain.

Brakspear Bitter
BITTER 3.4% ABV
An initial malt and well-hopped
bitterness develops into a bittersweet
and fruity finish.

Brakspear Special
STRONG BITTER 4.3% ABV
Full-bodied, with a hint of sweetness
and dry hop bitterness before finishing
citrus-fruity.

Brahma

Rua São Cristóvão, 1221, São Cristóvão, Rio de Janeiro, **BRAZIL**
www.brahma.com

The Portuguese brought beer to Brazil at the beginning of the 19th century but it was Swiss immigrant Joseph Villager who first brewed Brahma in 1888. Named after the Hindu god, Brahma has grown to be one of the world's most drunk beers. The company is now part of Anheuser-Busch InBev.

Brahma
LAGER **4.8**% ABV
Low in bitterness and light to drink, it has a subtle fruity aroma and no aftertaste.

Antarctica
LAGER **4.9**% ABV
Light in color, bitterness, and aroma, it is an easy drinking beer.

Braugold

Schillerstr. 7, 99096 Erfurt,
GERMANY
www.braugold.de

The brewery was founded in 1822, and acquired other breweries over time—up until 1948, the point at which it was nationalized by the GDR. After Reunification in 1990, Braugold was purchased by the Licher Privatbrauerei.

BREWING SECRET The brewers follow recipes from the famous Thüringer brewery.

Braugold Spezial
PILSNER 4.9% ABV
Has the typical golden color and dryness of a pilsner; highly aromatic with a balanced bitterness of hops on the palate.

Braugold Bock
BOCK 6.5% ABV
Its balanced, bitter aroma and strong flavor are typical of a bock.

Brewer's Art

1106 N. Charles Street
Baltimore, MD 21201, **USA**
www.thebrewersart.com

Housed in a grand 1902
townhouse in the Mount Vernon
area, The Brewer's Art serves
Belgian-inspired house beers and
an outstanding selection of
continental (primarily Belgian)
beers in a comfortable dining
atmosphere. It recently began
brewing and bottling some of
its beer under contract
in Pennsylvania.

Green Peppercorn Tripel
TRIPLE 10% ABV
Effervescent and full of life. Fruity and
spicy, a bit of candy sweetness, subdued
pepper, and a dryish finish.

Resurrection
DOUBLE 7% ABV
Caramel, dark fruits on the palate, and
surprising citrus notes. The yeast in the
first batch "died" and was "resurrected,"
hence the name.

BridgePort

1313 Northwest Marshall Street
Portland, OR 97209, **USA**
www.bridgeportbrew.com

BridgePort Brewing holds the
trademark of Oregon's Oldest
Craft Brewery, and its India Pale
Ale has come to define the
Northwest's beer character.
Despite several expansions,
it remains Portland-oriented. It
dedicates each release of Old
Knucklehead, its seasonal
barley wine, to a different
local personality.

India Pale Ale
INDIA PALE ALE 5.5% ABV
Citrussy from the outset. Solid malt
backbone, delicate fruits (peaches and
apples). Complex hoppy finish.

Black Strap Stout
STOUT 6% ABV
A rich blend of black strap molasses,
chocolate and coffee, finishing with
roasted bitterness.

Brinkhoff

Lütgendortmunder Hellweg 242,
44388 Dortmund, **GERMANY**
www.brinkhoffs.de

From its humble origins in 1844
as a small home brewery,
Brinkhoff has had more than 160
years of success, to become a
brand known far beyond its
hometown of Dortmund, one of
the beer capitals of the world.
Brinkhoff's No. 1 is a notable
name for every lover of the
special pilsners from this region.

Brinkhoff's No. 1

PILSNER 5% ABV
Typical bitter aromas of a pilsner.
Smooth, slightly sparkling, with
a golden-yellow color.

Brinkhoff's Radler

BEER BLEND 2.5% ABV
Honey-colored, sparkling, and pleasant
with citrus aromas; very refreshing and
not too sweet.

OREGON, USA

The term "Beervana" is often used to describe Oregon's culture of craft beer. Beer touring opportunities abound, and it would be possible to spend weeks traveling and never drink the same beer twice. This three-day trail starts in the seaside town of Newport, which is home to the iconic Rogue Ales brewery. It continues the next day with scenic stops on the way to Portland, then concludes with a full day in the Rose City. For more information visit www.oregonbeer.org.

1 DAY 1: NEWPORT AND ROGUE ALES

Rogue Ales Public House is located on OSU Drive, right in the center of the working seaport of Newport. There are plenty of bed and breakfasts to choose from in this friendly town, including Rogue's "Bed and Beer" apartments, above the public house. The public house is also the place to book in for one of the brewery tours, which commence at 3pm daily. *2320 OSU Drive, Newport (www.rogueales.com)*

2 DAY 2: PELICAN PUB & BREWERY

The scenic 48-mile (77-km) drive from Newport to Pacific City easily occupies a morning, so you should arrive just in time for lunch at the Pelican Pub & Brewery. The brewery-restaurant is located on the shoreline of Pacific City, where there are outstanding views of the oft-photographed Haystack Rock and Cape Kiwanda. *33180 Cape Kiwanda Drive, Pacific City (www.pelicanbrewery.com)*

3 DAY 2: GOLDEN VALLEY BREWERY & PUB

The scenic route to McMinnville passes through the Willamette Valley, one of the nation's premier wine-growing regions. The Golden Valley Brewery & Pub offers ales, sometimes aged in wine barrels. *980 East 4th St., McMinnville*

4 DAY 3: PORTLAND

With more than three dozen breweries in the metropolitan region, it is little wonder residents of Portland like to say they live in "Beervana." Here are some you could visit on Day 3 of this trail.

Hair of the Dog
This tiny brewery uses equipment not originally designed for brewing. Visits by appointment. *4509 SE 23rd Avenue, Portland (www.hairofthedog.com)*

Widmer (see p366)
Visit the brewery's Gasthaus restaurant to sample the full line-up of beers—including the Alt intended to be the brewery flagship before its Hefeweizen became an American standard. The brewery offers tours on Fridays and Saturdays. *929 North Russell, Portland*

BridgePort (see p84)
Oregon's oldest surviving brewery helped turn the Pearl District into a hip locale. *1313 Northwest Marshall Street, Portland*

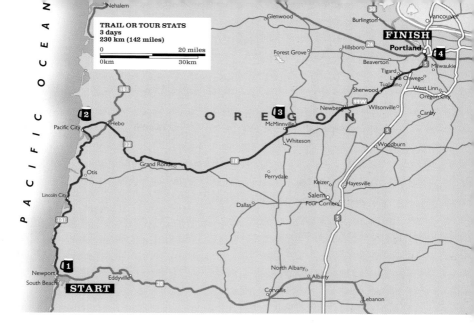

Higgins Brewpub
Greg Higgins uses local produce for his widely praised menu, which pairs well with Oregon beers and wines. *1239 SW Broadway, Portland*

Green Dragon Bistro and Pub
This relative newcomer quickly became an instant hit with a trendy crowd. Offers a constantly-changing selection of beers not necessarily found elsewhere, served by a knowledgeable staff. *928 SE 9th Avenue, Portland*

Horse Brass Pub
A Portland institution since 1976, the Horse Brass is a sprawling tribute to both the English pub and Oregon beer, offering 52 selections on draft. The pub is especially popular with the late-night crowd. *4534 SE Belmont Street, Portland*

Bristol

1647 South Tejon
Colorado Springs, CO 80906, **USA**
www.bristolbrewing.com

Since opening in 1994, Bristol
Brewing has been the beer hub in
Colorado Springs, as others have
come and gone. It ventured into
experimenting with barrels
ahead of many US breweries.

BREWING SECRET It has won awards
with a beer made using wild yeast and
lactic acid bacteria from raspberries
picked in nearby Cheyenne Canyon.

Winter Warlock

OATMEAL STOUT **6.5%** ABV
Toasted marshmallows and chocolate up
front, creamy chocolate and roasted
flavors on the palate.

Laughing Lab

SCOTTISH ALE **5.3%** ABV
Medium-bodied, with sweet notes of
caramel and toffee and a lingering
impression of smoke. Best on tap.

Brøckhouse

Høgevej 6, DK-3400 Hillerød,
DENMARK
www.broeckhouse.dk

A fast-growing and popular microbrewery to the north of Copenhagen, established in 2002. It was the goal of owner Allan Poulsen, a former IT engineer, to create something different from ordinary Danish pilsner.

BREWING SECRET Poulsen uses quality ingredients and British, German, and Belgian brewing traditions to create exciting and memorable brews.

Brøckhouse IPA
INDIAN PALE ALE **6%** ABV
Top-fermented ale brewed with three varieties of hops to achieve a sweet, balanced complexity.

Brøckhouse Esrum Kloster
ABBEY ALE **7.5%** ABV
Developed with the monks of Esrum Abbey. Strong nose; sweet, spicy flavor with hints of aniseed, lavender, rosemary, and juniper.

Brooklyn

1 Brewers Row
79 North 11th Street
Brooklyn, NY 11211, **USA**
www.brooklynbrewery.com

While Brooklyn Brewery pays homage to New York's rich brewing history, it is very much a 21st-century business, and occupies New York's first commercial building to derive all of its electricity from wind power. The brewery's bottled beers are made under contract in upstate New York, while brewmaster Garrett Oliver regularly produces seasonals and a reserve series at the brewery, sold on tap throughout the region.

Brooklyner Weisse

HEFEWEIZEN 5.1% ABV

Effervescent and banana-fruity from the start, backed up with spices, hops, and gentle clove notes.

Local 1

BELGIAN STRONG GOLDEN ALE 9% ABV

An explosion of aromas and flavors of fruits and spices, and a complex texture, all brought together with a chalky-dry finish.

Brouwerij 't IJ

Funenkade 7, 1018 AL Amsterdam,
NETHERLANDS
www.brouwerijhetij.nl

Amsterdam's favorite micro is
now the city's oldest brewery,
even though it was founded only
in 1985. Strong Belgian-style ales
form the backbone of the output,
though there's also a pils and a
witbier. Set in an old windmill,
the taproom is thronged on warm
summer afternoons, its outdoor
seating taken up by drinkers
enjoying the lowest beer prices
in Amsterdam.

Turbock
DOPPELBOCK 9% ABV
Packed with dark fruits and molasses
sweetness, the trademark Ij spiciness
adds a dimension not found in
German bocks.

Columbus
STRONG ALE 9% ABV
A balance of biscuity malt, coriander,
lemon, and resinous, minty hops.
Assertive, but not overpowering.

BrowArmia

Ul. Królewska 1,
Warszawa, 00-065, **POLAND**
www.browarmia.pl

Opened in 2005, this fine brewpub has a vibrant atmosphere—busy, convivial, and loud on music nights. Polish food with a modern twist is a specialty to match the beers on tap. Six beers are currently brewed in the smart cellar brewery, with six more planned for the future.

Pszenciczne
PALE ALE **4.8**% ABV
Not quite a Burton ale, it is strongly hopped in the kettle before being dry-hopped in the lagering tank.

Raspberry Wheat Beer
WHEAT BEER **5**% ABV
The house wheat beer is in the Bavarian style, with the addition of fresh raspberries. The fruit adds a refreshing, zesty tartness.

Bucher Bräu

Elsenthaler Str. 5-7,
9441 Grafenau, **GERMANY**
www.bucher-braeu.de

A medium-sized brewery that moved to the heart of the Bavarian Forest in 1982 after outgrowing its premises in the center of Grafenau. It has been owned by the Bucher family since 1863 (now in its fifth generation).

BREWING SECRET The natural cloudiness of the Hefeweizen comes from the yeast added at the time of bottling.

Grafenauer Hefeweizen
WHEAT BEER 5.2% ABV
Fresh and sparkling. The light taste of yeast is fine and aromatic. There is a little sweetness.

Helles
LAGER 4.9% ABV
Clear yellow beer, slightly bitter, with a reasonable sweetness, and a taste of the finest hops. A rather strong but rounded finish.

Budels

Nieuwstraat 9,
6020 AA Budel, **NETHERLANDS**
www.budels.nl

Budels is among the few
established, predominantly
bottom-fermenting Dutch
breweries. Started in 1870, the
business is currently run by the
fourth generation of the founding
Aerts family.

BREWING SECRET In recent years
Budels has diversified into top-fermenting
beers, such as kölsch, altbier, and an
abbey-style dubbel.

Budels Lager
PILS 5% ABV

A gentle, piney hop aroma is followed by
fruity, sweetish taste; perhaps closer to a
helles than a pils.

Budels Capucijn
ABBEY-STYLE DOUBLE 6.5% ABV

Sweet toasted malt aromas are
complemented by bitterness, dates, and
the merest hint of smoke.

Budweiser Budvar

Karolíny Světle 4, 370 21
České Budějovice,
CZECH REPUBLIC
www.original-budweiser.cz

The town of České Budějovice (Budweis) has been a home of brewing since 1265. Today, the Budějovický (Budweiser) Budvar product name has Protected Geographical Indicator status within the EU (like Cognac and Parma ham), but in the US, where Anheuser-Busch's Budweiser is trademarked, it is called Czechvar.

Budweiser Budvar / Czechvar

PREMIUM LAGER 5% ABV
Spritzy, with an attractive head, floral and grapefruit fruitiness on the nose, and a dry, biscuit malt palate.

Czech Dark Lager

DARK BEER 4.7% ABV
Its distinct malty flavor develops a cinnamon spiciness before rolling into biscuit undertones.

Caldera

540 Clover Lane
Ashland, OR 97520, **USA**
www.calderabrewing.com

Although it's been around since
1997, Caldera has enjoyed
increased visibility and
distribution since 2005, when it
became the first microbrewery in
Oregon to install a small-run line
for its distinctively packaged
canned beers.

BREWING SECRET Caldera sets itself
apart by continuing to use whole
hop flowers in all its beers.

IPA

INDIA PALE ALE **6.7**% ABV
Makes a large hop impression without
being heavy-handed. Citrus, pine, and
grapefruit from start to finish.

Pilsener

PILSNER **5**% ABV
Gets eight full weeks of lagering. Floral
aroma, with just an initial hint of sulfur,
with a crisp, hoppy flavor and finish.

Caledonian

42 Slateford Road, Edinburgh,
EH11 1PH **SCOTLAND**
www.caledonian-brewery.co.uk

The Caledonian attitude to
brewing beer is similar to that of
drinking it—the longer you've
been doing it, the more quality
you demand. It is the sole
survivor of some 40 breweries
that once resided in Edinburgh.

BREWING SECRET Caledonian is one of
the last breweries to use traditional
direct-fired coppers to boil the wort.

Caledonian 80 Shilling

SCOTTISH HEAVY **4.2% ABV**
Russett-brown and typically malt-led, with
an underlay of raspberry and a suggestion
of chocolate.

Deuchars IPA

INDIA PALE ALE **3.8% ABV**
A strident hop aroma, with citrus
notes and a degree of maltiness that
never wavers.

Cantillon

Gheudestraat 56, B1070 Brussel/
Anderlecht, **BELGIUM**
www.cantillon.be

As early as 1900, the Cantillon
family had beer blending
facilities here, in the old
southern suburbs of Brussels.
In 1970, Jean-Pierre Van Roy, who
had married Claude Cantillon,
took over the business, becoming
a staunch defender of old-style
brewing. His son Jean, however,
has shown in the last 10 years or
so that the brewery is not averse
to experimentation, on occasion
using fresh hops, and even
American "C-hops"—both
anathema to the lambic tradition.

Cantillon Gueuze
ORGANIC LAMBIC 5% ABV
Nose of citrus, horse blanket, wood, and
hay; woody flavors, with green fruit and
some sulfur; sour and tart in mouthfeel.

Lou Pepe Framboise
FRUIT BEER 5.5% ABV
A mix of lambic beer with a pure sugar
solution. One of the most intense fruit
beers on earth.

Capital

7734 Terrace Avenue
Middleton, WI 53562, **USA**
www.capital-brewery.com

Capital Brewery is known for its
excellent German-inspired
beers—brewed in copper kettles
from a defunct German
brewery—though some are made
with a twist. Autumnal Fire, for
instance, is a cross between a
doppelbock and an Oktoberfest-
style ale.

BREWING SECRET The grain for
Capital's Island Wheat is grown on an
island in Lake Michigan.

Munich Dark

DARK LAGER 5.4% ABV
Malt-accented, with early hints of caramel
and nuts. Building richness with
chocolate-toffee notes.

Special Pilsner

PILSNER 4.8% ABV
Light on the palate with a note of honey.
Lovely floral hop aromas and a sturdy
hop finish.

Captain Lawrence

99 Castleton Street
Pleasantville, NY 10570, **USA**
www.captainlawrencebrewing.com

Brewmaster-owner Scott Vaccaro represents the newest generation of American brewers, with a formal education in brewing science, then on-the-job training in the US and England. Back in his home state, he founded this brewery with the support of his family. He is at the forefront in experimention with barrel ageing.

Xtra Gold

TRIPLE 9% ABV
Citrus notes from Northwest hops blend seamlessly with juicy orchard fruits and a bit of candy sweetness.

Smoked Porter

PORTER 6.4% ABV
Smoky to start, but rich dark fruits, chocolate, and liquorice quickly emerge. Luscious palate.

Caracole

86, Côte Marie-Thérèse, B5500
Falmignoul, **BELGIUM**
www.brasserie-caracole.be

Started in around 1990, Caracole
moved after a few years from
Namur to the present location.
The brewery offers beers in
two varieties: a "normal," and
a "bio" (organic) version.
Caracole means "snail," and
production isn't rushed—but the
beers are enjoying growing
international recognition.

Troublette Bio

WITBIER 5% ABV
A fully organic Belgian white, with no
excess coriander, but a fine citrussy and
refreshing finish.

Nostradamus

BELGIAN DARK ALE 9.5% ABV
Caracole's strong dark ale is a mix
of roasted, fruity, malty, and higher
alcohol notes.

Carib

Eastern Main Road,
Champs Fleurs, **TRINIDAD**
www.caribbeer.com

The sole brewery on Trinidad since 1957, Carib has formed business links with InBev, Carlsberg, and Diageo—the owner of Guinness. The company also has breweries in Grenada, St. Kitts, and Nevis. The British brought commercial brewing to Trinidad just after World War I; the local taste favors sweet lagers and strong stouts.

Carib Lager

LAGER 5.2% ABV

Pale, but full-bodied with a rich head formation. Slightly aromatic, balanced between sweet and bitter.

Carib Stag

LAGER 5.9% ABV

European style lager. It is has a pale golden straw color with a rich head formation. Very sweet.

Cascade

131 Cascade Road, South Hobart,
Tasmania 7004, **AUSTRALIA**
www.cascadebrewery.com.au

Australia's oldest operating
brewery, complete with on-site
maltings, is also the most
striking, with the castellated
sandstone building nestled in the
foothills of the sometimes snow-
capped Mount Wellington. Now
part of the Foster's empire,
Cascade attracts tens of
thousands of beer lovers
annually to its visitor center.

Cascade Stout
MEDIUM STOUT **5.8% ABV**
Coffee notes up front, with milk chocolate
on the palate, followed by a moderately
bitter finish.

Cascade Blonde
SUMMER ALE **4.8% ABV**
Clean and crisp, with a hint of citrus
hop flavor.

Castelain

13 rue Pasteur,
62410 Bénifontaine, **FRANCE**
www.chti.com

Founded in 1926, this family brewery was passed into the hands of Yves and Annick Castelain from their parents in 1978. Under the name of Ch'ti (local patois for a northerner), they have developed a range of strong, mellow lager beers with a long, cold secondary fermentation period.

Maltesse
PREMIUM LAGER **7.7%** ABV
Blonde, rich, and strong, with a taste of barley, and an appealing hint of bitterness in the finish.

Ch'ti Blonde
LAGER **6.4%** ABV
Full-bodied, with just enough bitterness to be very refreshing. Mellow and tasty.

Castle / SAB

65 Park Lane, Sandown,
Sandtona, **SOUTH AFRICA**
www.sablimited.co.za

SAB—South African Breweries—
was founded in 1895 and began
producing its Castle Lager brand
in the mining town of
Johannesburg. The company
soon became the biggest brewer
in southern Africa. In 2002,
SAB bought Miller Brewing in
the US, and as SABMiller it has
become one of the biggest global
drinks companies.

Castle Lager
LAGER 5% ABV
Award-winning lager made from African
Gold Barley and Southern Star hops. It is
brewed in nine countries and sold in 40.

Castle Milk Stout
MILK STOUT 6% ABV
Dark, highly-hopped, strong stout with a
complex taste of roasted black malts,
coffee, and caramel.

Cereuro— Cervejeira Europeia

Estrada da Portela nº8,
2795 – 643 Carnaxide, **PORTUGAL**
www.sumolis.pt

Part of soft drinks manufacturer Grupo Sumol, this brewery was set up after the revolution of 1974, when the brewing industry was nationalized. It went into private ownership in the 1990s. The company also brews Magna, an interesting German-style dark beer, and markets Grolsch in Portugal.

Tagus
LAGER 5.4% ABV

A clear golden color, this beer is rich and malty with caramel overtones. Its estery nose hints of its alcoholic strength and its warming finish.

Cervesur

Av. De la Cultura 725, Cusco, **PERU**

Based in southern Peru in the Andes, the company, which is of German origin, has been brewing since 1898 and is now part of SABMiller. It is currently being merged with SABMiller's other Peruvian company Backus & Johnson. Its main brand, Cusqueña, is Peru's best-selling lager.

BREWING SECRET The water for brewing comes from a source high in the Andes.

Cusqueña
LAGER 5% ABV
Pronounced "Cus-Ken-Ya," the beer is crisp and refreshing, with a lingering lemon aroma.

Cēsu Alus

Aldaru laukums 1,
Cēsis, 4101 **LATVIA**
www.cesualus.lv

Cēsu Alus was founded in 1879
and is the oldest brewery in
Latvia. In 1999 it was purchased
by the Estonian brewer A. Le
Coq. It is now one of the largest
brewers in Latvia. It has a new,
state-of-the-art brewhouse and
further huge investment is being
planned. The town is renowned
for its beer festival, knights'
tournaments, and open-air
theater performances.

Cēsu Premium
LAGER **5.2%** ABV
Sweet chocolate taste with hints of
aromatic vanilla. In Latvia, balsam is
commonly used to flavor drinks.

Cēsu Balsam Porter
PORTER **6%** ABV
A pale golden color, it has hints of sweet
grass and hops on the nose.

Chimay

8, Route Charlemagne,
B6464 Baileux, **BELGIUM**
www.chimay.com

Though the bottling is done in
Baileux, the brewery is still in the
monastery at Forges-les-Chimay.
Since 1861, monks have brewed
here, but Chimay became the
leading Trappist brewery
through Père Theodore, who
went to Leuven University to
study brewing in a contemporary
way. Chimay never stopped
growing and is vital to the
economy of the region.

Chimay Tripel
ABBEY ALE 8% ABV
Sweet, grapey taste, with bittering hops
and herbal qualities; not entirely unlike a
dry white wine.

Grande Réserve / Bleue
BELGIAN STRONG ALE 9% ABV
Roasted malts, with some quite dominant
bitterness, and dark, ripe fruit (plums,
blue grapes), and pears.

La Choulette

18 rue des Écoles,
59111 Hordain, **FRANCE**
www.lachoulette.com

Founded in 1885, this farmhouse brewery is a rare survivor from the thousands of breweries that existed in the region in the late 19th century. Alain Dhaussy, the current brewer, has succeeded in creating artisan beers of real quality, faithful to the traditions of northern France, but with a real sense of innovation too.

Choulette Framboise
FRUIT BEER **6**% ABV
Refreshing, with a slight sourness. The note of ripe raspberries is present, but not too intrusive.

Porte Du Hainaut Ambrée
AMBER ALE **7**% ABV
Medium-bodied fruity beer, with flavors of cooked apples, pears, and caramel; slight bitterness.

Coopers

461 South Road, Regency Park,
Adelaide, South Australia 5010,
AUSTRALIA
www.coopersbrewery.com.au

While most Australian breweries
were progressively "lagerized"
during the 20th century, this
family-run Adelaide brewing
dynasty kept knocking out
cloudy, bottle-conditioned
ales and stouts. Since opening
a new expanded brewery in
2001, surging demand for their
beers has driven them to
become the country's third-
largest beermaker.

Coopers Sparkling Ale

AUSTRALIAN PALE ALE 5.8% ABV
Cloudy; fruity aromatics with a hint of
peaches; rounded, dry, yeasty finish.

Coopers Extra Stout

DRY STOUT 6.4% ABV
Espresso and bitter chocolate notes, with
banana hints too; robustly bitter finish.

Coors

311 10th Street
Golden, CO 80401, **USA**
www.coors.com

Although it merged with Molson, and that company now partners SABMiller in the US, Coors has continued to develop less mainstream beers. Its Blue Moon line competes with the largest craft brands, and its SandLot Brewery, within the Coors Field baseball stadium in Denver, regularly offers outstanding traditional lagers.

Blue Moon Belgian White

WITBIER 5.4% ABV

Citrussy sweet nose, spicy with notes of celery. Some wheat sourness, finishing on the sweet side.

Barmen Pilsner

PILSNER 5% ABV

Beautiful billowing head when poured correctly. Rich with Saaz hops, floral and spicy. Pleasantly grainy, with a long, bitter finish.

Cornelyshaff

Maison 37,9753 Heinerscheid,
LUXEMBOURG
www.cornelyshaff.lu

Situated in a nature park,
Cornelyshaff comprises a
popular bar, restaurant, and
hotel, as well as a brewery that is
open to visitors. It is modern,
gleaming, and energy efficient—
the cooperative that owns it
prides itself on minimizing its
environmental impact. The bar
and restaurant showcase the
beers and much farm produce
from the area.

Ourdaller Waïssen Tarwebier
WITBIER **4.6%** ABV
An unfiltered, cloudy wheat beer;
assertive in character, it is full of spice.

Kornelysbéier
RYE BEER **4.2%** ABV
A spicy aroma gives way to a strongly
flavored deep, earthy taste brought on by
the use of rye grain.

Crailsheimer Engelbräu

Haller Str. 29, 74564 Crailsheim,
GERMANY
www.engelbier.de

When this brewery was founded
by Georg Fach in 1738,
Crailsheim had 4,000 inhabitants
and 13 breweries. Fach was not to
know that his company would
become one of the most
successful in the country.

BREWING SECRET A survey of what
women like in a beer led to the creation of
the First Lady brand.

First Lady
DUNKLER BOCK 5.9% ABV
Mild, lightly bitter, and with
a harmonious malty aroma.

Kellerbier Dunkel
DUNKEL 5.3% ABV
Beautiful mahogany color; aromas of malt
and yeast; full-bodied, with a taste that is
both sweet and pleasantly bitter.

Creemore Springs

139 Mill Street, Creemore,
Ontario, L0M 1G0, **CANADA**
www.creemoresprings.com

Ownership by Molsons since
2005 has done little to lessen the
independence of this 100-year-old
brewery. The town of Creemore
nestles between the curiously
named Mad and Noisy rivers.
Every August the brewery
is a sponsor of a town-center
party called the Copper Kettle
Festival. Regular brewery tours
are run.

Premium Lager
LAGER 5% ABV
Soft malt and fruit flavors give way to
nutty overtones and a dry hoppy finish.

Urbock
BOCK 6% ABV
Dark brown, with a sweet, nutty texture;
fruit aromas can be found as the beer
warms in the glass.

Darmstädter

Goebelstr. 7, 64293 Darmstadt,
GERMANY
www.darmstaedter.de

The brewery stands next to the train station in Darmstadt—hence the train logo, used since 1847, and the animated steam engine on its website.

BREWING SECRET A revolution in the company's history was the complete change-over of all bottles to clip-tops in the year 2000.

Pilsner
PILSNER 4.8% ABV
A clear and elegant beer. A large amount of fine hops make this a typical pilsner: fresh and dry with a good bitter aroma.

1847 Zwickelbier
LAGER 4.8% ABV
Unfiltered and cloudy with subtle aromas of fine malt and a smooth, yeasty taste.

Darwin

Sunderland, Tyne & Wear,
SR1 2QE **ENGLAND**
www.darwinbrewery.com

The Darwin set-up is unique in that its commercial operation is complemented by a test brew plant based at the University of Sunderland. There, students on the Brewlab brewing sciences course are able to trial some 40 new beers each year. The best of them are then produced at the award-winning site.

Evolution Ale
BITTER 4% ABV
Light, clean, and satisfying, with a dry, hoppy character and layers of malt throughout.

Ghost Ale
BITTER 4.1% ABV
Golden and richly hopped, with citrus aromas dominating, followed by a well-balanced fruit piquancy.

Deschutes

901 Southwest Simpson Avenue,
Bend, OR 97702, **USA**
www.deschutesbrewery.com

What began with a brewpub in
1988 quickly expanded with a
separate production facility
that's grown into one of the
nation's largest craft breweries.
As well as selling a full line of
beers with notable hop character
throughout the western US,
Deschutes still operates its
original brewpub in downtown
Bend and another in Portland.
A Bond Street Series of special
beer releases, developed "at the
pub," has further widened the
brewery's portfolio.

Mirror Pond
PALE ALE 5.2% ABV
Grapefruit and fresh flowers at the outset.
Light, clean biscuit on the palate, with
generous hop flavor.

Inversion IPA
INDIA PALE ALE 6.8% ABV
A swirl of hop aromas (particularly
orange zest). Solid, biscuity malt holds
its own against bracing bitterness.

Desnoes and Geddes

214 Spanish Town, Kingston,
JAMAICA
www.jamaicadrinks.com

Now owned by global drinks giant
Diageo, Desnoes and Geddes was
established by two friends,
Eugene Desnoes and Thomas
Geddes, who set up a soft drink
plant in 1918 and began brewing
in 1927 with Red Stripe.

BREWING SECRET Red Stripe was
originally produced as an English ale.
It didn't become popular until it was
offered as a chilled lager instead.

Dragon Stout
SWEET STOUT 7.5% ABV
Having been primed with sugar on
bottling, the flavor is malty, with
a distinct note of molasses.

Dragon Gold
LAGER 5.5% ABV
Yellow in color, it has a grainy aroma,
a crisp, clean taste, and is best drunk
very cold.

Dětenice

Pivovar Dětenice, 507 24 Dětenice,
CZECH REPUBLIC
www.krcmadetenice.cz

The castle-based brewery—once
owned by the Prague chapter of
the Knights of Malta—closed in
1955 after several years of
nationalization, and reopened
only in 2000.

BREWING SECRET Beers are brewed
in direct-fired vessels and are filtered
through straw, fermented in wooden vats,
then lagered in oak barrels.

Svetlé Detenické Pivo 12°

PREMIUM LAGER 4% ABV

Aromatically floral, finely structured
body; sweet malt and honey influences,
and hoppy afterglow.

Tmavé Detenicke Pivo 13°

DARK BEER 4% ABV

A typically full-bodied dark lager;
malty, some spice, and faintly bitter
toward the finish.

Diebels

Brauerei-Diebels-Str. 1,
47661 Issum, **GERMANY**
www.diebels.de

Diebels was privately owned
from 1878 until 2001, when the
brewery was taken over by global
drinks giant InBev. The
Düsseldorfer Alt is the brewery's
most famous brand and is sold all
over Germany. Other, newer
brands include a pilsner and a
cola-blended beer called Dimix.

Diebels Alt
ALTBIER 4.9% ABV
Roasted malt aromas harmonize with a
sweet caramel taste; the finish is slightly
bitter from hops.

Diebels Pils
PILSNER 4.9% ABV
The full-body, light bitterness, and malt
aromas are typical of a pilsner, as is the
dark golden color.

Dinkelacker-Schwabenbräu

Tübinger Str. 46, 70178 Stuttgart,
GERMANY
www.ds-kg.de

Carl Dinkelacker was the first to brew pilsner in Stuttgart at the end of the 19th century, and his contemporary Robert Leicht was the first to deliver beer by car. Today, their breweries are in partnership and together form the biggest player in Baden-Württemberg.

Dinkelacker Privat
LAGER 5.1% ABV
A fine, smooth, and clear golden lager with a mild aroma of hops and a light note of malt.

Dinkelacker CD-Pils
PILSNER 4.9% ABV
Noble dry pilsner with strong aromas of hops and light malts; very harmonious and pleasant.

Distelhäuser

Grünsfelder Str. 3, 97941
Tauberbischofsheim, **GERMANY**
www.distelhaeuser.de

The Bauer family has owned this
brewery since 1876. It is situated
on the famous "Romantic Street"
in Tauberbischofsheim, which is
closely associated with the
German Romantic period. The
long-standing success of the
brewery is due to its attention
to quality over the course of
its history.

Distelhäuser Landbier
EXPORT 5.1% ABV
Malty aroma and a slightly caramel taste;
it has a mild sweetness and is rounded at
the finish. Sometimes described as a
"ladies' beer."

Distelhäuser Pils
PILSNER 4.9% ABV
Topped by a snow-white foam, this beer
has a harmonious bitterness and a great
aroma of hops.

Dithmarscher

Oesterstr. 18, 25709 Marne Holstein,
GERMANY
www.dithmarscher.de

This brewery, on the east coast of
Schleswig-Holstein, has been
operating for more than 230
years. It started as a small home
brewery; today it is bigger, but
the beers are still handmade.

BREWING SECRET The sparkle comes
from using the charmant method of
pressurized fermentation, and the
addition of dry, fresh carbonic acid.

Dithmarscher Dunkel
DUNKEL 4.9% ABV
This beer has a full-bodied charmant
character and a spicy taste with
notes of roastiness. A typical color:
dark mahogany.

Dithmarscher Pils
PILSNER 4.8% ABV
A mild and spicy beer, golden-yellow in
color, slightly sparkling.

Dixie

2401 Tulane Avenue
New Orleans, LA 70119, **USA**
www.distinguished-brands.com/
dixie.php

The 100-year-old Dixie Brewery
was the last survivor of New
Orleans' once-flourishing
brewing tradition, with some of
its beers aged in historic cypress
barrels. That is, until Hurricane
Katrina (and the subsequent
looters) devastated it in 2005. It's
not clear when it might reopen.
Meanwhile its beers are being
made at the Minhaus Craft
Brewery in Wisconsin.

Blackened Voodoo

SCHWARZBIER 5% ABV

In 1991, this dark lager was briefly
banned in Texas because of the voodoo
references on its label. Smooth and
light-bodied for southern drinking, with
chocolate and toffee notes throughout.

Döbler

Kornmarkt 6, 91438 Bad Windsheim,
GERMANY
www.brauhaus-doebler.de

Döbler celebrated its 140th
anniversary in 2007. Production
was traditional until 1950, after
which the brewery switched
to creating young-styled
beers using technologically
advanced equipment.

BREWING SECRET The barley has come
from sustainable sources since 1986.

Land Märzen
MÄRZEN 5.4% ABV
A very light märzen; dark yellow, with a
pleasant taste, not too sweet, but full-
bodied with a nice yeast finish.

Reichsstadtbier
KELLERBIER 5% ABV
Full-bodied, unfiltered, and cloudy, with a
taste of yeast. It is available on draft.

Dogfish Head

6 Cannery Village Center
Milton, DE 19968, **USA**
www.dogfish.com

Dogfish Head has found a
national audience for its "extreme
beers." These have included ales
developed using research from
archaeologists; recipes featuring
unusual ingredients, from
chicory to chilies; and beers that
simply have more of everything.
The brewery recently installed
the largest wooden brewing
vessels built in the US since
before Prohibition. Dogfish still
operates a brewpub in Rehoboth
Beach, where founder Sam
Calagione started in 1995.

Midas Touch
HISTORIC BEER 9% ABV
The ingredients—white Muscat grapes,
honey, and saffron—create layers of
flavor, melded with subtle acidity.

60 Minute IPA
INDIA PALE ALE 6% ABV
Flagship session beer brewed with
Warrior, Amarillo, and "Mystery Hop X,"
and brimming with citrus flavors.

De Dolle Brouwers

Roeselarestraat 12B,
B8600 Esen, **BELGIUM**
www.dedollebrouwers.be

By buying and renewing the old Costenoble Brewery in 1980, Kris Herteleer and his two brothers started, unknowingly, Belgium's microbrewery revolution. Fame soon reached international quarters—but then the "mad brewers" never searched for simplicity, a quiet life, or easy money. "Quality does the trick" is the motto of Kris—the only remaining brewer of the original three.

Oerbier

BELGIAN DARK ALE 9% ABV
Fruitiness throughout, from nose to finish. Very vinous character, grapey, and clearly strong in alcohol.

Arabier

SEASONAL CHRISTMAS ALE 12% ABV
Overripe grapes, raisins, and other dried fruits. Some hoppy bitterness hiding behind lots of sweet malts; acidic lining for a great balance.

Double Maxim

Hughton-le-Spring,
Sunderland, **ENGLAND**
www.dmbc.org.uk

After several years contracting
out the company's eponymous
beer, a new brewery was opened
in 2007 to cope with demand.
Bottling facilities are planned for
the near future.

BREWING SECRET Double Maxim uses
an original Vaux Brewery recipe, which
head brewer Jim Murray used when he
worked at Vaux in 1968.

Double Maxim
BROWN ALE 4.7% ABV
Caramel in the aroma; continues through
bittersweet flavors, then expands into
toffee notes.

Samson
BEST BITTER 4.6% ABV
A dependable northeast English
bitter, with a whiff of hop and a
malt-infused body.

Dreher

Magladi ut 17, Budapest, **HUNGARY**
www.dreher.hu

For many years this brewery was run by Anton Dreher, one of the great beer innovators. In the mid-19th century, he developed the technology to ferment beer at low temperatures and created a new kind of malty amber beer, called Vienna lager. For his achievements, Dreher was dubbed "The King of Beer." The company is now owned by SABMiller.

Dreher Classic
PILSNER 5.5% ABV

With a crisp, fresh aroma, this is a bitter, golden-yellow beer with an aroma of hops and a hint of malt.

Dreher Bak
DUNKLER BOCK 7.3% ABV

A rich, full-bodied dark beer, notes of caramel and malt, reminiscent of bittersweet chocolate.

Dubuisson

28, Chaussée de Mons,
B7904 Pipaix-Leuze, **BELGIUM**
www.br-dubuisson.com

Leuze is a town with three breweries, two of them in the Pipaix village. Dubuisson is probably the most dynamic, and its location, next to a major road, has made their brewery tap a very successful venture. The brewery excels in high alcohol ales, so extreme caution is advised when drinking these beers.

Bush Prestige
BELGIAN STRONG ALE **13% ABV**
This oak-aged version of the Ambrée is a true marvel in balance, despite its impressive strength.

Bush Ambrée
BELGIAN STRONG ALE **12% ABV**
In some markets known as "Scaldis," this is a treacherously drinkable alcohol-bomb.

Ducato

Via Strepponi 50/A, 43010 Roncole
Verdi di Busseto (PR), **ITALY**
www.birrificiodelducato.it

Young brewer Giovanni Campari
set up his microbrewery in 2007
near Giuseppe Verdi's birthplace,
not far from Parma. He proved
his skills from the outset,
brewing four beers full of
character. Further new lines
are confirming Ducato as one
of the most promising Italian
craft breweries.

New Morning
SAISON 5.6% ABV

Amazing saison, flavored with camomile
flowers. Easy-drinking and thirst-
quenching, with lovely earthy notes.

AFO
AMERICAN PALE ALE 5.2% ABV

AFO means "Ale For the Obsessed" and is
dedicated to hop lovers. Nice citrus fruit
aromas, caramel notes.

Duck-Rabbit

4519 W Pine Street
Farmville, NC 27828, **USA**
www.duckrabbitbrewery.com

Known for darkly intense beers,
this is one of several small
breweries that have thrived
since North Carolina changed
its law to allow beer stronger
than 6% ABV. Duck-Rabbit's
distinctive logo is based on an
illustration by philosopher
Ludwig Wittgenstein.

BREWING SECRET These quirky
brewers say "We sing softly to the yeast."

Baltic Porter
BALTIC PORTER 9% ABV
Caramel, toffee, blackcurrants, and other
dark fruits, perfectly blended. Smooth,
with restrained bitterness.

Milk Stout
STOUT 5.7% ABV
A well-integrated combination of roasted
coffee beans and chocolate, held together
by a creamy palate. Sweet, but not
too sweet.

Dugges Ale & Porterbryggeri

Möbelgatan 3, SE-43133 Mölndal,
SWEDEN
www.dugges.se

The brewery was founded in 2005 by Mikael Dugge Engström. His series of beers include Gothenburg, marrying old Swedish traditions with British and American inspiration, and Express Yourself, a collection of specialty brews with names like Holy Cow (an IPA) and Fuggedaboudit! (a brown ale).

Dugges Avenyn Ale

AMERICAN PALE ALE 5% ABV

Aromas of hops, flowers, and citrus fruits; flavors of grapes, pine, and a hint of caramel.

High Five!

INDIAN PALE ALE 7.5% ABV

Dark amber. Intense hop aroma; notes of strawberry jam, pine, and chocolate, and a dry bitterness.

Dupont

Brasserie Dupont, 5 Rue Basse,
B7904 Tourpes-Leuze, **BELGIUM**
www.brasserie-dupont.com

Western-Hainaut enjoys rich soil,
and farmsteads here were huge—
usually operating a brewery in
the winter, making beer to be
consumed on the land in summer
(hence the style of beer known as
saison). Brasserie Dupont became
solely a brewery, but owner Olivier
Dedeycker has re-engaged with
the history of the land, by
reintroducing farming and
cheese-making into this
marvellous brewery.

Avec Les Bons Vœux
SEASONAL WINTER ALE 9.5% ABV
Once a complimentary winter ale, but so
superb that it is now brewed year round.
Barnyard and earthy aromas mingle with
citrus zest. Grainy flavor: fresh white
bread with nuts, spices, and walnut oil.

Saison Dupont
SAISON 6.5% ABV
Formerly brewed in winter with the hot
summer months in mind—hence a dry,
refreshingly light brew.

BRUSSELS, BELGIUM

"B" is for Belgium, Brussels, and Beer. Today, Belgian beers can be drunk worldwide, but the very best place to embrace Belgian beer culture is in Brussels itself, with its unique cafés, bars, and brasseries.

1 TOONE

The Beer Temple (*Rue Marché Aux Herbes 56*) is one of the world's best beer shops. It stocks most of Belgium's artisanal brewers. It is close to a narrow alleyway that forms the entrance to Toone, a puppet theater with a bar. The walls of this hidden gem are adorned with staring marionettes and the atmosphere is as good as the Kwak beer served here—in the correct glass of course.
6 Impasse Schuddevelde, off 21 Petit Ruedes Bouchers, Brussels

2 GRAND PLACE

Brussels' famous Grand Place is home to the Belgian Brewers Association and Brewery Museum—both occupy the opulent Brewers House. Several bars surround the square, but there are even better places to drink nearby. In September the square hosts an annual beer festival.

3 POECHENELLEKELDER

Opposite one of the world's most improbable tourist attractions, the Manneken Pis, is the Poechenellekelder. Loved by the people of Brussels, the bar has a list of 90 fine beers—a perfect introduction to the world of Belgian beers.
5 Rue du Chêne, Brussels

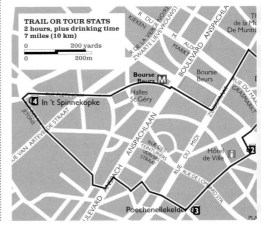

TRAIL OR TOUR STATS
2 hours, plus drinking time
7 miles (10 km)

| 0 | 200 yards |
| 0 | 200m |

4 IN 'T SPINNEKOPKE

Away from Grand Place, but not too far, can be found In 't Spinnekopke. "The Little Spiders Head" is a small, intimate two-bar restaurant and café. It is as Bruxellois as you can get and has to be one of the best places in Brussels to eat and drink beer. Chef Jean Rodriguez prides himself on pairing food and beer superbly. *1 Place du Jardin aux Fleurs, Brussels*

5 DELIRIUM

Ilot Sacré is a clamor of medieval lanes and fish restaurants with outrageous menu boards, and energetic and sometimes insistent waiters trying to coerce people inside to dine. Down one such alley is Delirium. Don't wait at your table for service, go to the bar, which claims to stock more than 2,000 beers. *4a Impasse de la Fidélité, Brussels*

6 MORTE SUBITE

Along the road is Galeries Royales St Hubert. Once the world's largest covered shopping mall, it leads the way to Morte Subite—a magnificent Art Nouveau bar, which is said to be the best surviving fin-de-siecle long bar in the world. Here is the place to try wildly fermented lambic or gueuze beers with a plate of *tête pressée* (brawn) or *kip kap* (pig cheeks). *7 Rue Montagne aux Herbes Potageres, Brussels*

7 BIER CIRCUS

Up the hill from Central Station is Bier Circus. This is the place to seek out beers from Belgium's growing band of artisanal brewers and experience the creative diversity of Belgian brewing. But take some friends with you—many of the beers are served only in 75cl bottles. *89 Rue de l'Enseignement, Brussels*

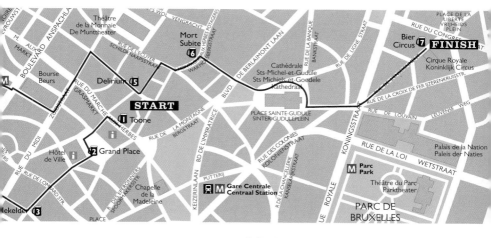

Duvel Moortgat

Breendonkdorp 58-66, B2870
Breendonk-Puurs, **BELGIUM**
www.duvel.be

Started as a small family brewery, Moortgat continued producing top-fermented ale at a time when everywhere lager reigned. The Moortgat ale evolved into the iconoclastic Duvel, a beer that has become so popular that the brewery group renamed itself. Moortgat now owns breweries in Belgium and abroad.

Duvel
BELGIAN STRONG ALE 8.5% ABV
Sometimes dubbed "red," to distinguish it from the filtered version, this ultra dry ale hides its potency as no other.

Maredsous 8°
BROWN ABBEY ALE 8% ABV
Arguably the best from the Maredsous Abbey range. Estery, fruity notes, and tobacco leaf.

Duyck

113 route Nationale, 59144 Jenlain,
FRANCE
www.duyck.com

Originally a farmhouse brewery,
Duyck was established in 1922,
producing beers in the northern
bière de garde style—brewed
and bottled in the winter for
laying down and drinking in
the summer. In the 1950s, the
family began bottling their
beers in recycled champagne
bottles. Raymond Duyck,
the present manager, is the
fourth generation of this family
of brewers.

Jenlain Ambrée
AMBER ALE 7.5% ABV
Full-bodied, with a hint of bitterness,
the mellowness of roasted malt and
aromas of stewed prunes and caramel.
A perfect accompaniment to food, but
also an ingredient in rustic local dishes
such as *Carbonnade Flamande* (beef
cooked in beer).

Echigo

3970 Fukui, Nishiura-ku, Niigata
City, Niigata 953-0076, **JAPAN**
www.echigo-beer.jp

The brewers of the venerable
Tsurukame saké of Niigata
opened Japan's first
microbrewery in February of 1995
to great fanfare. Operations have
expanded from the original
brewpub to a large-scale brewery
with canning line today. While the
canned products are well
regarded, the more expensive
small-production bottled products
are even more highly prized.

Echigo Pilsener

PILSNER 5% ABV

This reasonably priced craft beer has
a rich malty flavor, moderate bitterness,
and a clean, quick finish.

Echigo Stout

STOUT 7% ABV (PREVIOUSLY 5%)

Higher gravity and more care in
the brewing of this beer results
in a brilliant interplay of rich,
roasty flavors.

Eel River

1777 Alamar Way
Fortuna, CA 95540, **USA**
www.eelriverbrewing.com

Eel River had been around less than five years when, in 2000, it became the first certified organic brewery in the US. The brewpub added a production brewery in nearby Scotia in 2007, moving into an abandoned mill. The new brewery is 100 percent powered by biomass—that is, mill waste such as wood chippings, and spent grain from brewing.

Organic Porter
PORTER 6.3% ABV
Malty and creamy with chocolate aromas and flavors, and lesser notes of roast coffee beans. Robust.

Triple Exultation
OLD ALE 9.7% ABV
Not organic. A complex nose of rich caramel-toffee and fruit, then piney hops assert themselves.

Eggenberg

Eggenberg 1,
A-4655 Vorchdorf, **AUSTRIA**
www.schloss-eggenberg.at

Schloss Eggenberg is a small castle in Upper Austria that has been brewing for more than 500 years. A broad range of lagers (including a non-alcoholic one) are produced for the local market, and some fine bock beers are brewed for export; these include an urbock and even a blonde version of the traditionally dark Samichlaus beer.

Samichlaus
DOPPELBOCK 14% ABV
Intense malt aroma, with noticeable alcohol. Sweet and fruity (dried cherries, figs, and plums); very little hop character present.

Hopfenkönig
PILSNER 5.1% ABV
Very pale, with a firm head and haylike spicy hop aromas. Light body followed by some dry bitterness.

Eggenberg

Latrán 27, 38115, Český Krumlov,
CZECH REPUBLIC
www.eggenberg.cz

Nowhere but in Bohemia could
two towns merge over brewing
disputes. Years of arguing about
wheat beer privileges were
resolved simply by uniting
neighbors Latrán and Krumlov,
and establishing a single
brewery. Over time, the brewery
passed from the Eggenberg
family to the Schwarzenbergs
and down the centuries to its
present owners, Dionex.

Eggenberg Světlý Ležák
PREMIUM LAGER 5% ABV
Powerfully floral with sweet butterscotch
notes; zesty, firm, and delightfully
balanced to a bitter finish.

Eggenberg Tmavý Ležák
DARK BEER 4.2% ABV
Deep and dark, with a hop pungency,
then a malty caramel and toffee
bittersweet palate.

Einbecker

Papenstr. 4, 37574 Einbeck,
GERMANY
www.einbecker.com

The story goes that, in 1521, Martin Luther said that Einbecker's beer was his favorite. In 1612, Bavarian dukes engaged a master brewer from Einbeck, whose beer eventually became known as bock, in a corruption of the name Einbeck.

UR-Bock Hell
BOCK **6.5%** ABV
The pale malt and fine hops give this classic bock a hearty taste.

Einbecker Spezial
EXPORT **5.2%** ABV
Has the typical golden-yellow color of an export beer. Has a fine, slightly sweet flavor.

Emerson's Brewery

14 Wickliffe Street, Dunedin,
NEW ZEALAND
www.emersons.co.nz

New Zealand's most awarded micro offers an enviable portfolio of year-round beers, as well as seasonal specialties such as Taieri George, a spiced dark ale, and a US pale ale featuring American hops.

BREWING SECRET Emerson's delightful session beer called Bookbinder Bitter is available only on tap.

Emerson's Old 95

BARLEY WINE 7% ABV
Robust bottle conditioned ale, with rich, toffeelike malt and resiny hops. Will reward careful cellaring.

Emerson's Organic Pilsner

NEW WORLD PILSNER 4.9% ABV
Bursting with passion fruit and citrus. A showcase for New Zealand's Riwaka hop variety.

Erdinger

Lange Zeile 1+3, 85435 Erding,
GERMANY
www.erdinger.de

This is the biggest and most famous specialist wheat beer brewery in the world. The first mention of a brewery at Erding was in 1886, but it was not until 1949 that the name Erdinger Weissbräu was used.

BREWING SECRET Fresh spring water and hops from the Hallertau region are used in brewing.

Erdinger Pikantus
DARK WEIZENBOCK 7.3% ABV
Normally a wheat bock is sweet, but not so Erdinger's. Watch out for the ABV on this one.

Erdinger Schneeweisse
WINTER BEER 5.6% ABV
Darker and heavier bodied than the normal weizen. It is available between October and February.

Everards

Castle Acres, Narborough,
Leicestershire, LE19 1BY **ENGLAND**
www.everards.co.uk

After brewing his first pint in
1849, William Everard stated his
intention, and one that the
fifth-generation family is proud
to uphold: "No effort shall be
found wanting in the production
and supply of genuine ale of
first-rate quality." Integrity
remains king today.

BREWING SECRET Fuggles and
Goldings are the key hops here.

Tiger
BITTER 4.2% ABV
Some spicy hop and caramel on the nose.
Classically bittersweet palate, with a
rounded toffeeness.

Original
STRONG BITTER 5.2% ABV
Copper-hued, full-bodied, and a toasted
caramel aroma beckoning port wine and
fruit flavors.

Exmoor

Wiveliscombe, Somerset,
TA4 2NY **ENGLAND**
www.exmoorales.co.uk

Exmoor was among the first wave
of microbreweries in the early
1980s. Its fundamentals have
never altered from a reliance on
skills, investment in innovation,
and adherence to the principles
of small-batch brewing. Being
Somerset's largest brewery
positions it as a regional
producer, and the potential of its
backbone brands is still to be
fully capitalized upon.

Exmoor Gold

BITTER 4.5% ABV
Powerful earthy hop, lemon, and juicy
malt aromas; fruity, butterscotch
sweetness, and memorable finish.

Exmoor Ale

BITTER 3.8% ABV
Medium-bodied, with some malt and hop
in the aroma and bitter hop aftertaste.

Fantôme

8, Rue Préal, B5454 Soy-Erezée,
BELGIUM
www.fantome.be

Dany Prignon started this
micro in a shed in the Ardennes,
and while today he exports
his beers to many countries,
the shed is still the brewery's
home—though it now contains
far more equipment.

BREWING SECRET More works of art
than products of brewing science, many
of the beers are never brewed the same
way twice.

Black Ghost
BELGIAN STRONG DARK ALE 8% ABV
One of the few regularly seen: malty, with
fruity depths, but also flavors of cypress
and pine.

Fantôme
SAISON 8% ABV
The brewery's staple blonde beer:
fruity, lactic, variable, and in the style
of a saison.

Fässla

Obere Königstr. 19-21, 96052
Bamberg, **GERMANY**
www.faessla.de

In 1649, just a year after the end
of the Thirty Years' War, master
brewer Hans Lauer founded this
brewery in Bamberg. In modern
times, 1986 was a turning point,
when the Kalb family took over
control. Fässla's specialty beers
are well known in the region.

BREWING SECRET Bambergator is the
strongest beer brewed in Bamberg.

Lagerbier
LAGER 5.5% ABV
Strong yellow in color; fine, compact
foam; sparkling. Full-bodied and slightly
malty with a light bitter taste.

Bambergator
DOPPELBOCK 8.5% ABV
A dark brown, full-bodied, and very strong
doppelbock, bursting with harmonious
hop bitters.

Faust

Hauptstr. 219, 63897 Miltenberg,
GERMANY
www.faust.de

A typical regional family-run
company. The brewery is about
350 years old and changed hands
many times in the first 200 years
of its history. The Fausts took
over in 1895, and still own it
today. There are many different
styles of beer produced, some of
which have won prizes.

Schwarzviertler
DUNKEL 5.2% ABV
Dark, roasty, and slightly smoky. There is
also caramel and a little bitter-chocolate
on the tongue. It is full-bodied and has
a dry finish.

Faust Kräusen
KELLERBIER 5.5% ABV
A mild, full-bodied beer with a light note
of honey; it is very fresh.

Felinfoel

Llanelli, Carmarthenshire,
SA14 8LB **WALES**
www.felinfoel-brewery.com

Sitting astride the Liedi River
and leaning heavily on the
industrial traditions of south
Wales—and its workers' thirsts—
Felinfoel Brewery has been in
existence since 1878. It is famed
for producing Britain's
first canned beer in 1935.
Extensive modernization came in
the 1970s, but Felinfoel is still
family-owned.

Double Dragon
BITTER 4.2% ABV
Invitingly rich in color, malty and subtly
hopped, with an evenly balanced,
full-drinking nature.

Cambrian Bitter
BITTER 3.9% ABV
Labeled "a good, honest Welsh bitter," the
bitter is full-flavored, with balanced malt
and hop aromas.

Fiege

Moritz Fiege, Scharnhorststr. 21-25,
44787 Bochum, **GERMANY**
www.moritzfiege.de

"We are a classic regional
brewery" says Hugo Fiege, the
boss of the company. He sees his
brewery as an ambassador for the
Ruhr region. It is an institution
offering typical local beers—
inhabitants of the Ruhr love their
beer. There is little chance of a
big global player acquiring Fiege.

Moritz Fiege Pils
PILSNER **4.9**% ABV
A classic pilsner with bitter aromas of
good hops, a light malty taste, and a fine
dry structure.

Schwarzbier
SCHWARZBIER **4.9**% ABV
Elegant and with a malty sweetness, this
coffee-colored beer has light bitter
aromas of fine hops.

Finlandia

Suokulmantie 237, Matku,
Forsaa FI-31110, **FINLAND**
www.finlandiasahti.fi

Finlandia is a specialist brewer
of *sahti*, a traditional Finnish
home-brew made with rye and
other grains, flavored with
juniper twigs and berries. Beer
enthusiasts can sample Finlandia
Sahti in Helsinki at St. Urho's
Pub and the Restaurant Savotta.
The best time to do so is during
Helsinki's Sahti Week, which
takes place in May each year.

Sahti Strong

SAHTI 10% ABV

Sweet and somewhat oily on the palate;
the juniper nose gives way to a
bubblegum aftertaste.

Tavallinen

SAHTI 8% ABV

A deep chestnut color, with a heavy
juniper nose and a hint of blackcurrant.

Flensburger

Munketoft 12, 24937 Flensburg,
GERMANY
www.flensburger.de

Five citizens of Flensburg
founded this brewery in 1888.
During the 1970s, the brewery's
reputation was enhanced when a
comedian kept referring to a
"Flasch Flens" in his act. The
term came to be used for a bottle
of Flensburger, which at the time
was the only German beer to use
clip-top bottles.

Flensburger Pils
PILSNER 4.8% ABV
A typical golden pilsner—malty,
refreshing, and with slightly bitter
aromas of hops in the finish.

Kellerbier
KELLERBIER 4.8% ABV
Amber and cloudy, like all kellerbiers, the
Flensburger version is full-bodied and
tastes naturally fresh, slightly sweet, and
has a dry finish.

Flossmoor Station

1035 Sterling Avenue
Flossmoor, IL 60422, **USA**
www.flossmoorstation.com

Brewers Matt Van Wyk and Andrew Mason have expanded on what barrel-ageing pioneer Todd Ashman started at Flossmoor Station Brewing. They offer a wide range of award-winning beers in a pub housed in a former train station. The brewery recently launched a small range of bottled beers.

Pullman Brown Ale
BROWN ALE 7% ABV
Brewed with hand-toasted malts and molasses. A full-bodied blend of chocolate, toffee, and dark fruit.

De Wilde Zuidentrein
SOUR ALE 7% ABV
A Flanders brown ale, aged in an oak wine barrel on fresh raspberries for a year, dosed with wild yeasts.

Flying Dog

2401 Blake Street
Denver, CO 80205, **USA**
www.flyingdogales.com

With labels by British illustrator
Ralph Steadman, and the "gonzo"
spirit of the late Hunter S.
Thompson (both friends of
founder George Stranahan),
Flying Dog is not your average
brewery. The original brewpub
was founded in Aspen but is now
headquartered in Denver, while
the company moved brewing
operations to Frederick in
Maryland in 2008.

Gonzo Imperial Porter
PORTER 9% ABV
Rummy, chocolatey, and almost sweet
before dry cocoa flavors and solid hop
bitterness kick in.

Doggie Style Pale Ale
PALE ALE 5.3% ABV
A fragrant mixture of fresh fruits to start.
Citrus accentuates fruit in the middle,
well balanced by biscuity malt. Clean,
dry finish.

Flying Fish

1940 Olney Avenue
Cherry Hill, NJ 08003, **USA**
www.flyingfish.com

Flying Fish Brewing began worldwide and then went local. It started out as a "virtual brewery" on the Internet before establishing itself as a distinctly regional brewery in 1996, now serving a 100-mile (160-km) radius around its South Jersey home. The brewery recently increased capacity, with plans to widen the range of beers on offer.

Belgian Style Dubbel
DOUBLE 7% ABV
Chocolate mingled with dark fruit, and a pleasant whiff of alcohol. Finishes on the sweet side of dry.

ESB Ale
EXTRA SPECIAL BITTER 5.5% ABV
Malt-accented, rich with caramel and fruit character, and with an underlying nuttiness. Hops are American, but restrained.

Forstner

Dorfstrasse 52, A-8401 Kalsdorf
bei Graz, **AUSTRIA**
www.hofbraeu.at

One of the more adventurous
new brewers, Gerhard Forstner
has recently made inroads into
brewing Belgian and American-
style ales. His brewery is in an
old farmhouse building that has
also served as a school. Some of
his beers are endorsed by the
Slow Food movement and are
sold at Slow Food festivals.

Styrian Ale
BITTER ALE 5.6% ABV
Very dark burgundy; roasty and fruity
(grapefruit?) aromas; slightly tart and very
refreshing, with a medium bitterness.

Triple 22
BELGIAN STYLE TRIPLE 9.5% ABV
Copper, with firm head and aroma of
pawpaw and mango. Sweet and full-
bodied; spicy and bitter finish.

Freeminer

Cinderford, Gloucestershire,
GL14 3JA **ENGLAND**
www.freeminer.com

Anyone born in the Forest of
Dean who has worked in a coal
mine for a year and a day may
open his own mine. Few such
mines remain, but Freeminer
celebrates this heritage with
its ales.

BREWING SECRET Freeminer ales are
made from traditional malt varieties and
whole Worcestershire hops in open-
topped fermenters.

Speculation
STRONG BITTER 4.8% ABV
An initial chocolate sweetness is
replaced by a hoppy rush and rich
malt flavor layer.

Freeminer Bitter
STRONG BITTER 4.8% ABV
Distinctly bitter and abundantly hoppy,
balanced by a malt character that denotes
"no-nonsense" beer.

Freiberger

Am Fürstenwald, 09599 Freiberg,
GERMANY
www.freiberger-bier.de

This brewery was the first in
Sachsen to produce a pilsner.
Other exclusive beers followed:
Freiberger Silberquell (1903) and
a wheat beer (1909). The
Eichbaum brewery in Mannheim
has acquired Freiberger and is
focusing on making it one of
the most modern beer producers
in Germany.

Jubiläums-Festbier

MÄRZEN 5.8% ABV
With aromas of malt and a very fine taste
of hops, this amber-colored beer is
pleasant and full-bodied.

Schwarzes Bergbier

SCHWARZBIER 4.7% ABV
Deep black, with fresh, malty aromas.
Full-bodied and precisely balanced
between malts and hops.

Friedenfels

Schlossbrauerei Friedenfels,
Gemmingenstr. 33, 95688
Friedenfels, **GERMANY**
www.schlossbrauerei-friedenfels.de

The brewery is situated in the
southern part of the largest forest
in Europe, between Oberpfälzer
Wald and Fichtelgebirge.
Friedenfels is the leading
brewery of the region.

BREWING SECRET The pure springs of
the national park have helped Friedenfels
to produce excellent beers for more than
100 years.

Friedenfelser Pils Leicht
LIGHT BEER 2.8% ABV
This reduced-alcohol beer is golden and
on the dry side, with aromas of fine hops
in the finish.

Friedenfelser Weizen Leicht
LIGHT WHEAT BEER 2.7% ABV
This light beer is fermented in the bottle.
Its taste is a mixture of bitter hops and
sweet barley and wheat—typical of
the style.

Freistädter

Promenade 7, A-4240 Freistadt,
AUSTRIA
www.freistaedter-bier.at

The town of Freistadt lies close to
Austria's border with the Czech
Republic, and its brewery is
owned by the townspeople. Since
1777 every owner of a building
inside the old city walls
automatically owns a certain
number of shares of the brewery;
those shares can be sold only
along with the building itself.

Rauchbier
SMOKED LAGER 5.3% ABV
Pale amber, with a smoky nose; dry and
aromatic, with a nice balance of smoked
malt and hops.

Ratsherrn Trunk
EXPORT 5.1% ABV
A firm head and a full body. Low hop
bitterness, with a hint of grass in
the aftertaste.

Füchschen

Ratinger Str. 28, 40213 Düsseldorf,
GERMANY
www.fuechschen.de

Altbier has been a favored brew
at Füchschen since 1848. The
fourth generation of the family
is in charge. There have been
some changes since 1995,
including the installation of
new brewing equipment.

BREWING SECRET The Düsseldorf
carnival in February is a good
opportunity to sample the altbier.

Füchschen Alt

ALTBIER 4.5% ABV
Dark mahogany in color, this typical
Düsseldorfer is malty with a very
intense aroma of hops. Slightly
carbonated, and fresh.

Silberfüchsen

WHEAT BEER 5.4% ABV
A northern-style wheat beer, less sweet
than its Bavarian counterpart. Smooth,
fruity, and sparkling.

Fuller's

Chiswick Lane South, London,
W4 2QB **ENGLAND**
www.fullers.co.uk

London's last remaining
traditional family brewer,
Fuller's has been based at the
historic Griffin Brewery near the
Thames River in Chiswick since
1845. Brewing on the site,
however, goes back 350 years.
Despite its global prominence,
Fuller's retains a small company
spirit and formidably energetic
outlook. Its beers have received
countless awards, notably the
Campaign For Real Ale
Champion Beer of Britain, which
it has won five times.

London Pride
BITTER 4.1% ABV
A fruity sweet malt nose and a floral
spiced hop presence with marmalade
undercurrents.

ESB
EXTRA SPECIAL BITTER 5.5% ABV
Complex aromas, with the house-style
orange fruit complementing tangy hops
and roasted malt.

Full Sail

506 Columbia Street
Hood River, OR 97031, **USA**
www.fullsailbrewing.com

Full Sail represents much that is
new in American brewing.
Founded in 1987, it became
employee-owned in 1999, and its
beers reflect an independent
nature. The core brands (Amber,
IPA, and Pale Ale) reach a wide
audience in 15 western states.

BREWING SECRET The brewery also
offers seasonals that bear the LTD (Living
the Dream) label and a bolder series of
Brewmaster's Reserve beers throughout
the year.

Amber
AMBER ALE 5.5% ABV
Citrus and spice, quickly balanced by
underlying sweetness. Seamless through
to a clean finish.

Session Lager
US LAGER 5.1% ABV
Designed as a throwback to beer
produced before Prohibition, with
appropriately retro packaging. Clean and
malt-accented.

Fürstenberg

Postplatz 1-4, 78166
Donaueschingen, **GERMANY**
www.fuerstenberg.de

Count Heinrich I von
Fürstenberg was granted the
right to brew beer in 1283, but it
was not until 300 years later that
a proper brewery was built.
Fürstenberg was a major brewery
by the beginning of the 20th
century.

BREWING SECRET The beers are made
with water from the Black Forest and
yeast from Donaueschingen.

Fürstenberg Gold

LAGER **4.9%** ABV
Smooth, with few aromas of hops. This
clear golden beer is a bit sweeter than the
usual lager.

Fürstenberg Hefe Dunkel

DUNKEL **5.4%** ABV
Chestnut in color, and sparkling;
harmonious with a malty aroma and light
caramel sweetness, yet strong in the
mouth.

Fürstlichen Ellingen

Schloss-Strasse 19, 91792 Ellingen, **GERMANY**
www.fuerst-carl.de

Owner Carl Friedrich Fürst von Wrede is a direct descendant of Napoleon's field marshal Carl Philipp, Prince of Wrede. The brewery opposite his castle in Ellingen was founded in 1690, but the brewing history of Ellingen is certainly older. The beer has been called Fürst Carl for about 200 years.

Fürst Carl Josefi Bock

BOCK **7% ABV**
A creamy, malty, and full-bodied beer, with a velvet and silky texture.

Fürst Carl Urhell

LAGER **4.6% ABV**
The clear yellow color is typical for a lager; the taste is pleasant and not too dry, with very little sweetness.

Galbraith's

2 Mt. Eden Road, Mt. Eden,
Auckland, **NEW ZEALAND**
www.alehouse.co.nz

Located in a former library, New
Zealand's first real ale brewpub is
best known for its home-brewed
English style ales—all served by
hand pump. Visitors can also
enjoy an excellent Abbey-style ale
and a couple of flavorsome lagers,
as well as a fine range of imports
and craft beers from other New
Zealand brewers.

Bellringers Bitter

ENGLISH BEST BITTER 4.5% ABV
Copper colored ale with a biscuity,
toffeelike palate, plenty of earthy hops,
and an appetizingly dry finish.

Bob Hudson's Bitter

ENGLISH BITTER 4% ABV
A full-flavored session bitter very much in
the vein of the English pale ale Timothy
Taylor's Landlord.

Gayant

63 Faubourg de Paris,
59500 Douai, **FRANCE**
www.brasseurs-gayant.com

Established in 1919, this
independent, family-owned
brewery has always embraced
and pioneered new styles of
brewing, from ales made
using the top-fermentation
technique, to Celta, the first
non-alcoholic beer.

BREWING SECRET Brasseurs de Gayant
brews the strongest beer in France, called
Bière du Démon (12% ABV).

La Goudale
ALE 7.2% ABV
Golden, dense, and full of malty aromas,
with a slight bitterness imbued by the
Flemish hops.

Amadeus
WHEAT BEER 4.5% ABV
Cloudy and pale yellow, this is a light and
refreshing beer, with aromas of citrus
fruit and coriander.

Gilde

Hildesheimer Str. 132,
Hanover, **GERMANY**
www.gildebrau.de

It was about 500 years ago that
Cord Broyhan presented his beer
to the people of Hanover.
Broyhan—a pale style of wheat
beer—was popular for centuries
in the city. Gilde, Hanover's
longest-surviving brewery,
now owned by InBev, was
founded in 1870.

BREWING SECRET A modern version of
broyhan is exported to the US.

Ratskeller Premium Pils
PILSNER 4.9% ABV
A dry, golden-yellow pilsner; full-bodied,
typical bitterness of hops, and a
nice finish.

Lindener Special
EXPORT 5.1% ABV
The most successful export beer of
Niedersachsen has a golden color and
tastes pleasant with smooth yeast-flower
flavors in the mouth.

Girardin

Lindeberg 10-12,
1700 Sint-Ulriks-Kapelle, **BELGIUM**
www.brouwerijgirardin.com

As rural as you can get, Girardin is still very much a farm and brewery, and this authentic lambic brewer and gueuze blender has no time for curious visitors. If, however, you come simply to stock up on lambic—as the locals and other blenders do—the brewers will gladly help you to their citrussy, spontaneously fermented brews.

Faro Girardin

BLENDED LAMBIC 5% ABV

Caramel, meaty, and woody aromas; slight sour edge around the caramel. Filtered, as the yeast would wreak havoc with sugars from the syrup.

Girardin Fond Gueuze

GUEUZE 5% ABV

This delectable unfiltered gueuze has a marked grapefruit flavor.

Glaab

Frankfurter Str. 9, 63500
Seligenstadt, **GERMANY**
www.glaabsbraeu.de

For more than 250 years this
brewery has been owned by the
Glaab family. It was founded in
1744 and became known for its
wide variety of beers and for
Vitamalz, the biggest German
brand of pure malt drinks. The
company is the only private
brewery in the Offenbach region,
to the south of Frankfurt.

1744
KELLERBIER 5.3% ABV
This cloudy, amber-colored beer is
Glaab's youngest product. The taste of
fine malt is typical.

Dunkles
DUNKEL 5.3% ABV
Clear amber-colored beer in which the
light bitterness of hops is prominent. A
great dunkel with a nice malty finish.

Goose Island

1800 West Fulton Street
CHICAGO, IL 60612, **USA**
www.gooseisland.com

This brewery's extensive range reflects the MBA (Master of Beer Appreciation) Program that it established shortly after opening as a brewpub in 1988. When Goose Island built its production brewery in 1995, brewmaster Greg Hall would launch dozens of styles during the course of a year. Goose Island still operates the original pub on Clybourn as well as another near Wrigley Field, and both still offer an "MBA" (actually a kind of loyalty card!).

India Pale Ale
INDIA PALE ALE 5.9% ABV
Pineapple and grapefruit, full of hop flavor, with a fruit and malt back-bone balancing the bitterness.

312 Urban Wheat
US WHEAT BEER 4.2% ABV
Typically unfiltered and hazy, with a citrussy, almost sweet, hop nose that announces it is American. Tart, fruity, with underlying creaminess.

Gourmet-bryggeriet

Bytoften 10-12,
DK-4000 Roskilde, **DENMARK**
www.gourmetbryggeriet.dk

One of the largest microbreweries in Denmark, "The Gourmet Brewery" creates specialty beers that are designed to be paired with food. The brewery's partner is a trained chef who works together with a local restaurant to create recipes that are attached to 66cl bottles for sharing. The company recently acquired the Ølfabrikken Brewery.

Ølfabrikken Porter
PORTER 7.5% ABV
Black as the night, with a thick head of foam. Intense body with coffee, chocolate, and liquorice notes.

Gourmetbryggeriet Bock
DOPPELBOCK 7.2% ABV
Deep reddish in color, with a heavy aroma of malt and caramel backing up the strong body.

Great Divide

2201 Arapahoe Street
Denver, CO 80205, **USA**
www.greatdivide.com

Opened in 1994, Great Divide Brewing quickly earned a reputation for carefully balanced beers. Its ales have grown bigger (in strength and hop character), and the brewery's reputation has grown, but its beers still retain that delicate equilibrium. The brewery is a short walk from Coors Field, home of the Rockies baseball team.

Hibernation Ale
OLD ALE 8.1% ABV
A complex, earthy nose packed with chocolate, roasted nuts, and freshly baked molasses cookies—flavors just keep emerging.

Titan IPA
INDIA PALE ALE 6.8% ABV
Balanced, in a big way, with plenty of caramel-sweet body to match the piney, grapefruity hops throughout.

Great Lakes

2516 Market Avenue
Cleveland, OH 44113, **USA**
www.greatlakesbrewing.com

Selling its beer across a growing
region, this brewery has been an
industry leader in tracking the
quality of its beer on retailers'
shelves. Its brewing complex
always merits a visit. The original
1988 brewpub sits across from
the production brewery, which
came online in 1998. Visitors are
directed to the taproom's striking
Tiger Mahogany bar and shown
bullet holes reputedly made by
Eliot Ness, the "untouchable"
Prohibition agent who brought
down gangster Al Capone.

Edmund Fitzgerald Porter
PORTER 5.8% ABV
Perfectly balanced, chocolate-mocha
throughout, delightful fresh quality, and a
dry coffee finish.

Eliot Ness
VIENNA LAGER 6.2% ABV
Bold and hoppy in the Vienna style, with
creamy, nutty maltiness and brisk
hoppiness nicely balanced.

Green Flash

1430 Vantage Court
Vista, CA 92081, **USA**
www.greenflashbrew.com

Green Flash refers to a rare light
phenomenon that lasts only
seconds at sunrise or sunset over
water. Green seems appropriate
for a brewery gaining a national
reputation for its hop-accented
beers, although brewer Chuck
Silva has proved adept at a wide
range of styles.

West Coast IPA

INDIA PALE ALE 7% ABV
Northwest hops balanced on a solid malt
base. Earthy, floral, citrussy, piney,
grapefruity, and bitter.

Nut Brown Ale

BROWN ALE 5.5% ABV
Deep brown, with nuts and cocoa from the
outset, and more chocolate and caramel
on the palate. Subdued, earthy hops.

Greene King

Bury St. Edmunds, Suffolk,
IP33 1QT **ENGLAND**
www.greeneking.co.uk

After more than 200 years,
Greene King has developed into a
formidable and dynamic force in
the British brewing industry.
Benjamin Greene opened his
brewery in 1799 and it merged
with the rival King Brewery in
1887. The company has in recent
years acquired several of its
competitors—namely, Morland,
Ruddles, Ridley's, and Hardy &
Hanson—and closed them amid
some controversy. Belhaven of
Dunbar was another recent
acquisition, it being bought
up in 2005.

Abbot Ale
STRONG BITTER 5% ABV
A biscuit malt and spicy hop aroma, with a
tangy and bittersweet fruit and malt palate.

IPA
INDIA PALE ALE 3.6% ABV
Distinctly copper-colored, with
a clean, fresh hop savoriness and subtle,
sweetish malty nose.

Grünbach

Kellerberg 2, 85461 Bockhorn,
GERMANY
www.schlossbrauerei-gruenbach.de

Grünbach has had a host of
owners, including the famous
Paulaner and Erdinger
breweries. Alexander Noll is
currently at the helm.

BREWING SECRET Grünbach's Benno
Scharl wheat beer carries the name of an
18th-century Bavarian master brewer who
wrote an influential textbook on brewing
techniques.

Altweizen Gold
WHEAT BEER 5.3% ABV
Clear golden and finely balanced between
yeast and carbonic acid, with a lightly
sparkling, dry freshness.

Benno Scharl
WHEAT BEER 5.3% ABV
Yellow, and clouded with yeast, Benno
Scharl tastes mild and sweet, pleasant
and well balanced.

Guinness

St. James's Gate, Dublin 8,
IRELAND
www.guinness.com

When you can make a virtue out of the time it takes to pour a pint—119.5 seconds to be precise—you know you have no ordinary beer in your hands. Guinness defines stout, Ireland, and Irishness, but it is also inextricably linked with innovation in physics, chemistry, packaging, and advertising. 250 years after young Arthur Guinness's first mash, it is brewed in 50 countries worldwide and enjoyed in 150.

Guinness Original
STOUT 4.2% ABV
The packaged version's coffee and cream aroma highlights fruit, chocolate, and some late hoppiness.

Foreign Extra Stout
SPECIAL STOUT 7.5% ABV
Leafy hop aroma, with burnt toast, rich malt, bitter coffee, and liquorice flavors ripening effortlessly.

Haake-Beck

Am Deich 18/19, 28365
Bremen, **GERMANY**
www.haake-beck.de

Founded in 1826, the Haake-Beck brewery is one of the most famous in northern Germany. Milestones in the company's history include the creation of Haake-Beck Kräusen Pils and the first Maibock in 1950. It is part of the InBev stable today.

BREWING SECRET Haake-Beck's sister is the famous Beck's label, which is exported by InBev around the world.

Haake-Beck 12
EXPORT 5% ABV
This is a new Haake-Beck. A harmonious, golden beer, with a level of sweetness that is often liked by women drinkers.

Edel Hell
LAGER 4.7% ABV
A mild alternative to the pilsner: not so dry, a little bit sweet, and golden like a typical lager.

Haandbryggeriet

Thornegaten 39,
N-3015 Drammen, **NORWAY**
www.haandbryggeriet.net

This small brewery is known
for its hand-made brews and for
keeping Norwegian brewing
traditions alive. Housed in a
200-year-old wooden building,
it is run by volunteers, and
experimentation is encouraged.

BREWING SECRET As well as using old
oak wine barrels, they are now ageing
beer in former Akevitt spirit casks.

Dark Force
WHEAT STOUT **9**% ABV
Uses wheat and dark roasted malts and
house wheat yeast. High hop aroma and
ample bitterness.

Norwegian Wood
TRADITIONAL ALE **6.5**% ABV
Made from naturally smoked Munich,
Crystal, and chocolate malts; spiced
with locally gathered juniper twigs
and berries.

Hacker-Pschorr

Hochstr. 75, 81541 München,
GERMANY
www.hacker-pschorr.de

Hacker-Pschorr is one of the
most traditional breweries in
Munich, and its restaurant is a
tourist attraction, especially
during Oktoberfest. Beer
production was mentioned for
the first time here in 1417.

BREWING SECRET The Purity Law and
principles of long lagering are followed;
there are no preservatives or additives.

1417
KELLERBIER 5.5% ABV
Naturally cloudy, unfiltered, with
a dull golden color. Low carbonic acid
makes it very smooth.

Superior
MÜNCHNER SPECIAL 6% ABV
The clear, amber-colored Superior is
based on an old recipe and has a malty,
aromatic taste, without too many hops.
Highly drinkable.

Hair of the Dog

4509 Southeast 23rd Avenue
Portland, OR 97202, **USA**
www.hairofthedog.com

Chef-turned-brewer Alan Sprints
founded this tiny cult brewery in
1994. His first ale, Adam, was
brewed in the Adambier style of
Dortmund in Germany, and
based on the research of beer
writer Fred Eckhardt.

BREWING SECRET Every bottle carries
a batch number. Check the website to
match it to brewing and bottling dates.

Adam
STRONG ALE 10% ABV
Rich and complex, with dark fruits, bread,
chocolate, smoked peat, and more, all
cleverly unified.

Fred
STRONG ALE 10% ABV
Named after Eckhardt, this beer defies
categorization. Dark fruits and juicy ones,
spices and hops—impossible to
summarize.

Hakusekikan

5251-1 Hirukawa Tahara,
Nagatsugawa, Gifu 509-8301, **JAPAN**
www.hakusekikan-beer.jp

One of Japan's most distinctive breweries, Hakusekikan pushes the envelope of possible beer styles. Head brewer Satoshi Niwa is brilliant and imaginative, experimenting with wild beers using airborne yeast, while also making use of long fermentation times, barrel ageing, and other methods to produce truly distinctive beers.

Super Vintage
STRONG ALE **14.3%** ABV
Astonishingly fruity and complex beer, yet boasts a surprisingly dry finish. Permanently on tap at Beer Club Popeye in Tokyo.

Smoked Pale Ale
PALE ALE 5% ABV
A session pale ale given just a hint of smoked malt, with the smoky flavor appearing only in the finish.

Hambleton

Holme-on-Swale, North Yorkshire,
YO7 4JE **ENGLAND**
www.hambletonales.co.uk

A million-pound investment has resulted in a completely new brewery for Hambleton, with state-of-the-art bottling facilities. Innovation has been at the heart of the operation since 1991, as evident in the label designs and bespoke brewing equipment. Several awards, including one for a gluten-free range, have been well deserved.

Stallion
BITTER 4.2% ABV
For some, a true Yorkshire bitter, with its malty character, nuttiness, and enhanced hopping rate.

Nightmare
PORTER 5% ABV
An extra-stout porter that uses a combination of four malts for a massively complex flavor.

Harpoon

306 Northern Avenue
Boston, MA 02210, **USA**
www.harpoonbrewery.com

This brewery, with major
facilities in Boston and Vermont,
has tapped into specialty-beer-
drinkers' affection for hops, with
its flagship IPA accounting for 60
percent of sales. However, its
wheat-based UFO has recently
been the fastest-growing brand,
and its 100 Barrel Series of
one-offs guarantees there's
always something new.

IPA

INDIA PALE ALE **5.9% ABV**
Floral at the outset; zestful citrus aromas.
More hops in the flavor, biscuitlike palate,
subdued bitterness at the end.

Munich Dark

DUNKEL **5.5% ABV**
Rich, almost sweet, with hints of toast,
then chocolate. Restrained hops and a
long, smooth finish.

Harvey's

Lewes, East Sussex,
BN7 2AH **ENGLAND**
www.harveys.org.uk

The seventh generation of John
Harvey's descendants are still
involved in this prime example of
Victorian Gothic-style brewery
grandeur. The tower and
brewhouse dominate the skyline,
and the fermenting rooms and
cellars remain structurally
unaltered, although they now
house a modern plant with
equipment that has increased
production enormously.

Blue Label
PALE ALE 3.6% ABV
Deliciously full-bodied though fairly low
in alcohol, with a whiff of leafy hop and
sweet malt counterbalance.

Armada Ale
BEST BITTER 4.5% ABV
Amber colored, with a well-balanced
combination of fruit and hops on
the palate.

Harviestoun

Alva, Clackmannanshire,
FK12 5DQ **SCOTLAND**
www.harviestoun-brewery.co.uk

The brewers of Harviestoun say
they can't pretend it's a job—it's
their work, but also their play
and their passion. Curiosity
toward flavors and aromas wrung
from natural ingredients was the
brewery's mission in 1985, when
the business was originally set
up, and a move to a purpose-built
plant with fresh investment has
resulted in national accolades.

Bitter & Twisted
BITTER **4.2**% ABV
Ripe grapefruit and lemon-influenced
hop aromas are anchored by a
distinct maltiness.

Schiehallion
PREMIUM LAGER **4.8**% ABV
Cask lager, brewed with Bavarian hops
for a delightful nose. A rigid maltiness
prevails throughout.

Hawkshead

Staveley, Cumbria,
LA8 9LR **ENGLAND**
www.hawksheadbrewery.co.uk

The focus at Hawkshead is on
traditional beer styles that have
been given a modern twist. A new
20-barrel (3,200-liter) brewhouse
was fitted out in 2006—an
integral feature is a farm gate for
leaning on contemplatively. The
brewery's public beer hall, where
award-winning ales are served, is
a magnificent showcase for the
beers and their provenance.

Hawkshead Red
RED ALE **4.2%** ABV
A bittersweet red ale, malty and spicy on
the palate, with juicy, woody aromas.

Hawkshead Gold
BEST BITTER **4.4%** ABV
Hoppy and uncompromisingly bitter, with
complex fruit flavors from its English and
American hop blend.

Herold

262 72 Březnice, **CZECH REPUBLIC**
www.heroldbeer.com

The town's Baroque castle
is fully restored, and its
attached brewery continues
to produce pilsner-style beers
in a traditional, hand-crafted
manner to a "small is beautiful"
philosophy. The range includes
wheat beers and Bohemian
Black Lager.

BREWING SECRET Open fermenters,
home-drawn water, and resident maltings
accentuate its heritage.

Bohemian Black Lager

DARK LAGER **4.1**% ABV

A schwarzbier-type lager; bitter chocolate
flavors, plus a little malty sweetness, and
a long, dry, slightly smoky finish.

Premium Bohemian Lager

PREMIUM LAGER **5.1**% ABV

Full-bodied, yet softly textured,
with a classic creamy malt veil
and late hop dryness.

Herrngiersdorf

Schlossallee 5, 84097 Herrngiersdorf,
GERMANY
www.schlossbrauerei-
herrngiersdorf.de

Herrngiersdorf is situated
between Regensburg and
Landhut, in the middle of
Niederbayern. With more than
875 years of history behind it,
this is the oldest private brewery
in the world. It has been owned
by the Pausinger family since
1899. Since 1995 the sixth
generation of the family has been
managing it.

Sündenbock

BOCK 7.3% ABV
A typical dark doppelbock with
a light taste of caramel; very full-bodied
and sweet in the finish.

Publiner

DUNKEL 4.9% ABV
This beer is very dark and has a
strong taste, with very roasty malt
aromas and light bitters of hops.
(The Irish would love it...)

High Falls

445 St. Paul Street
Rochester, NY 14605, **USA**
www.highfalls.com

High Falls is still brewing old-style Genesee beers on the site where they have been made since 1878. It also makes the J.W. Dundee family of beers for the traditional ale market.

BREWING SECRET High Falls is one of the largest and oldest continuously operating breweries in the US.

Genesee Cream Ale
CREAM ALE **4.9%** ABV
Pale, faintly sweet, with roast corn flavors; smooth and easy to drink.

JW Dundee's IPA
INDIA PALE ALE **6.3%** ABV
A seasonal summer beer. Relatively sweet caramel character, with more bitterness than flavor from its hops. Crisp finish.

Hite

640, Yeongdeungpo-Dong,
Yeongdeungpo, Seoul,
SOUTH KOREA
www.hite.com

Founded in 1933 as Chosun
Breweries, Hite is Korea's
leading brewer, with 60 percent
of local sales. Carlsberg is a
substantial investor in the
brewery. The present production
at Hite amounts to approximately
150 million gallons (seven
million hectoliters) per annum.
The company also makes a
rice-based wine.

Hite
LAGER **4.5%** ABV
Golden in color, Hite is a light,
easy drinking beer—with an aroma
of bubblegum.

Prime Max
LAGER **4.5%** ABV
Pale orange in color; with a sweetcorn
aroma, it has hints of biscuit and
citrus fruits.

Hoegaarden

Stoopkensstraat 46,
B3320 Hoegaarden, **BELGIUM**
www.inbev.com

Although this is now a brand in the portfolio of brewing giant InBev, it is the lifeblood and spirit of Pierre Celis, Belgium's preeminent brewing revolutionary, that still haunts this brewery. Proof of this came in 2007, when InBev's moguls wanted to close the plant: fate, however, obliged them to reverse their decision.

Hoegaarden Wit

WITBIER 4.9% ABV

From as early as the 18th century, the town of Hoegaarden was importing blue Curaçao oranges. The peel was mixed with coriander seeds, and, as the rich soil of the area yielded lots of wheat, a very distinct, fruity, and spicy style of beer evolved.

Hofbräu München

Hofbräuallee 1,
81829 München, **GERMANY**
www.hofbraeuhaus.com

The Hofbräuhaus in Munich is
a very famous restaurant,
frequented by visitors from
around the world. It was founded
in 1607 by Maximilian I, Duke
of Bavaria. The linked brewery
is situated in Riem, outside of
the city.

BREWING SECRET The water used to
brew Hofbräu is drawn from a depth of
490 ft (150 m).

Hofbräu Original
MÜNCHNER HELLES 5.1% ABV
This clear golden beer is refreshing and
dry, with a harmonious balance of malt
and hops.

Hofbräu Dunkel
DUNKEL 5.5% ABV
This is the oldest type of Bavarian beer,
dark amber in color, and full of fine flavor
and enticing malt aromas.

Hog's Back

Tongham, Surrey,
GU10 1DE **ENGLAND**
www.hogsback.co.uk

Established in 1992, the Hog's
Back brewhouse takes up part of
an 18th-century farm. Steady
expansion, extensions to storage
facilities, and re-equipping the
fermenting room have continued
since, and many awards have
been gathered along the way.

BREWERY SECRETS "Late hops" are
added at the end of the boil, contributing
additional fragrance to the beer.

Traditional English Ale / TEA
BEST BITTER **4.2% ABV**
Well-crafted, with delicate, fruity aromas,
some bittersweet malt flavoring, and a
long, dry finish.

Hog's Back Bitter
BITTER 3.7% ABV
A biscuit-influenced session bitter, with a
fragrantly aromatic citrus fruit and light
malt afterglow.

Holden's

Woodsetton, Dudley, West Midlands,
DY1 4LW **ENGLAND**
www.holdensbrewery.co.uk

Third and fourth-generation
family members are very much
involved in the Holden's
business, which started life in the
1920s with a brewpub, before
expanding next door into a neatly
tiled brewery on two floors.

BREWING SECRET The mild uses a mix
of amber malt, caramalt, and black malt,
along with Fuggles hops.

Holden's Golden
BITTER 3.9% ABV
Fuggles hops and Maris Otter malt
combine in this medium-bodied, straw-
hued pale ale.

Black Country Mild
MILD 3.7% ABV
Bold chestnut red, with nutty biscuit
notes and wrappings of chocolate,
caramel, and earthy hops.

Holt

Cheetham, Manchester,
M3 1JD **ENGLAND**
www.joseph-holt.com

A family business survivor in an
increasingly corporate sector,
Holt's admits—with some pride—
to being unashamedly old-
fashioned. That does not mean
backward-looking, however, and
its well-structured projects and
clear vision have brought steady
expansion to the brewery and to
its portfolio of 127 pubs.

Holt 1849

BEST BITTER 4.5% ABV

A 150-year anniversary ale, with a
vibrant and generous celebratory hop
flavor to match.

Holt Bitter

BITTER 4% ABV

Spicy hops dominate the aroma with tart
fruitiness tempered by biscuit malt and
bittersweet fruit.

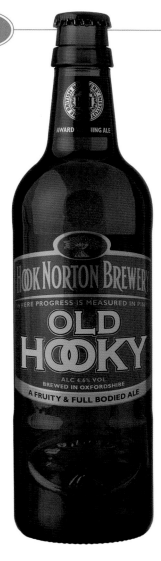

Hook Norton

Banbury, Oxfordshire,
OX15 5NY **ENGLAND**
www.hooky.co.uk

A particularly striking example
of a Victorian tower brewery,
Hook Norton is partly powered
by steam, via a series of belts,
cogs, and shafts. Drays pulled by
shire horses deliver to local pubs,
further demonstrating how the
brewery likes to preserve
traditional practices. While doing
this, Hook Norton also produces
some of the country's most
outstanding ales.

Old Hooky
STRONG BITTER 4.6% ABV
Beautifully poised, with a piquant, fruity
nature and malt character rounding off a
bitter finish.

Hooky Bitter
BITTER 3.6% ABV
Subtly hoppy on the nose, then malt
and fruit appear, before a returning
hop finish.

COTSWOLDS, ENGLAND

The village of Hook Norton in north Oxfordshire is the perfect base for any visitor exploring the Cotswolds or the city of Oxford. For the traveler, three of the village's pubs—the Sun, the Pear Tree, and the Gate Hangs High—all offer accommodation.

DAY 1: **HOOK NORTON BREWERY**

This is a near-perfect example of a Victorian tower brewery. It is still powered by a steam engine, and the making of Hook Norton's beers is a tactile, aural, and visual experience. Only the finest malted barley is used in the mash tun, and this needs to be manually removed when the wort is drained off the grist. The seemingly magical transformation of turning sweet wort into alcohol takes place in the brewery's hard-working open fermenters. A horse-drawn dray still delivers beer to local pubs. The Visitor Center is open from Monday to Saturday, though tours of the brewery must be booked beforehand via the website. The tour is followed by some sampling of Hook Norton beer. *Brewery Lane, Hook Norton (www.hooky.co.uk)*

DAY 2: **WYCHWOOD BREWERY**

The drive from Hook Norton to Witney takes in some glorious countryside, and at the end of the trip is the Wychwood Brewery. Tours of the brewery can be booked online. They last for two hours and go through the brewing process for Wychwood and Brakspear beers, from raw ingredients to the finished product. The tour takes in Brakspear's famous "Double Drop system" fermenting vessels. *Eagle Maltings, The Crofts, Witney (www.wychwood.co.uk)*

THE KING'S HEAD INN

Before returning to Hook Norton, pass by Cotswold Brewing (www.cotswoldbrewing company.com) at Foscot. Unusually for a British micro, brewer Richard Keene makes continental-style lagers. With a meandering stream at its side, the King's Head Inn, at nearby Bledington, is the perfect place to drink a glass of Cotswold Brewing's beer. *The King's Head Inn, The Green, Bledington (www.thekingsheadinn.net)*

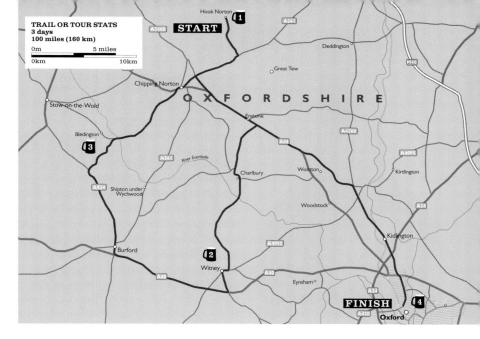

TRAIL OR TOUR STATS
3 days
100 miles (160 km)

0m — 5 miles
0km — 10km

START

Hook Norton

Deddington

Great Tew

Chipping Norton

O X F O R D S H I R E

Stow-on-the-Wold

Enstone

Bledington

3

River Evenlode

Charlbury

Wootton

Kirtlington

Shipton under Wychwood

Woodstock

Kidlington

Burford

2

Witney

Eynsham

FINISH

4

Oxford

 DAY 3: **OXFORD**
The third day of the trail offers a chance to sample some of the fabulous pubs in the historical city of Oxford—a place where good beer, culture, and a convivial atmosphere sit cosily together.

The Bear
Small and friendly, The Bear is on a narrow lane between Christ Church and Oriel colleges. It claims to be the oldest pub in Oxford, and is built on the site of a former bear-fighting pit. The walls are decorated by a collection of 5,000 ties. *6 Alfred Street, Oxford*

King's Arms
The King's Arms sits at the end of Broad Street, which is famous for its colleges and bookshops. The large pub is a warren of rooms and is much loved by locals and students. *40 Holywell Street, Oxford*

Turf Tavern
Hard to find but worth the search, the Turf Tavern is built on the only remaining part of the city wall. It sells a fabulous collection of British beers. *Bath Place, Holywell, Oxford; for directions go to the pub's website: www.theturftavern.co.uk*

Eagle & Child
Near Oxford's dreaming spires and the Ashmolean museum, Eagle & Child was a haunt of writers J.R.R. Tolkien and C.S. Lewis, who belonged to a literary group in the 1930s and 40s called the Inklings. *49 St. Giles, Oxford*

Hop Back

Downton, Salisbury, Wiltshire,
SP5 3HU **ENGLAND**
www.hopback.co.uk

Having soon outgrown its humble 1980s pub-cellar beginnings at the Wyndham Arms in Salisbury, Hop Back developed and expanded through a series of premises for brewing and drinking its beers, picking up significant awards along the way. At the core of the range is the multi-award-winning Summer Lightning.

Summer Lightning
STRONG BITTER 5% ABV
Intensely bitter, with a grassy, fresh, hoppy aroma and some malt lingering on the palate.

Crop Circle
BITTER 4.2% ABV
Cleverly blended aroma and bittering hops combine with corn nuances for a delicate fruity crispness.

Hopworks / HUB

2944 SE Powell Boulevard
Portland, OR 97202, **USA**
www.hopworksbeer.com

Hopworks Urban Brewery is the
first brewery in Portland to offer
only organic beers, part of its
commitment to "green culture."
HUB's founder-brewmaster
Christian Ettinger made
Portland's first organic beers.

BREWING SECRET HUB fires its
brewing kettle with bio-diesel fuel.

Velvet ESB
SPECIAL BITTER 5.2% ABV
A session ale by American standards; rich
in caramel, soft on the palate, with
signature hop character throughout.

Organic IPA
INDIA PALE ALE 6.6% ABV
Fresh hop aromas—pine, grapefruit,
lemon zest. Hop flavors, bitterness
matched by bright malt character.

Hue

243 Nguyen Sinh Cung
Hue City, **VIETNAM**

The Hue Brewery is based in Hue City, the old capital of Vietnam, on the banks of the famous Perfume River in central Vietnam. Carlsberg—which entered Vietnam in 1993 with the acquisition of a 60 percent stake in South East Asia Brewery, based in the north of the country—now has a 50 percent share in the Hue Brewery.

Hue

LAGER 5% ABV

A yellow corn color with a thin white head, and the body seems somewhat thin too. It is an easy-drinking beer, without surprises and a nose with hints of toast. Not much complexity, but a refresher nonetheless.

Huvila

Puistokatu 4, FI-57100,
Savonlinna, **FINLAND**
www.panimoravintolahuvila.fi

This craft brewery, making British-style ales, *sideri* (cider), and *sahti*, is located in Savonlinna, a popular tourist area in the Lake Saimaa area. The complex offers good food at the brewery-restaurant Huvila, bed and breakfast, live music, brewery tours, and a brewing school.

BREWING SECRET All of Huvila's products are unfiltered.

Huvila Porter
PORTER 5.5% ABV
English roasted malts give a strong coffeelike, roasted aroma with a hint of chocolate.

Huvila ESB
STRONG BITTER 5.2% ABV
Robustly hopped with a fruity and floral aroma, complex flavors, and a long and bitter aftertaste.

Hydes

46 Moss Lane West, Manchester, M15 5PH **ENGLAND**
www.hydesbrewery.com

Hydes is another of those remarkable family-owned breweries that has carved out a niche in its home region. Hydes Original has persevered with the same recipe and exacting standards that were applied on day one—back in 1863. The business continues to face the future with enthusiasm and in confident style.

Hydes Original
BITTER 3.8% ABV
A northwest classic: copper-colored, full-bodied, with a distinctive bittersweet flavor.

Dark Mild
MILD 3.5% ABV
A fruit and malt nose and complex flavorings that meander through berry fruits, malt, and chocolate.

Ilzer Sörgyár

Ilzer Sörgyár Rt.,
2200, Monor, **HUNGARY**
www.ilzer.hu

Located 22 miles (35 km) south of
Budapest, this brewery was
founded in the early 1990s. Its
range of brews now includes Alt
Bayersicher Dunkel, a dark
wheat beer; Diet, a beer that
is low in sugar; and a kosher beer
called Shalom.

BREWING SECRET Ilzer developed and
brewed the first Hungarian wheat beer.

Ilzer Hefeweissbier
WHEAT BEER 5% ABV
Cloudy yellow, with a wispy white head.
Hints of banana and spice give way to a
citrussy finish.

Ilzer Roggen Rozs Sör
RYE BEER 4.8% ABV
Hazy to the eye, this is a complex rye beer
of some originality. The rye imparts rich
spice notes.

Iron Hill

Various locations in Delaware and Pennsylvania, **USA**
www.ironhillbrewery.com

Named after a Revolutionary War landmark in Delaware, the Iron Hill Brewery & Restaurant chain continues to grow throughout Delaware and Pennsylvania, offering a set line-up at each location but also a range of specials. Its brewers also package an Iron Hill Reserve Line in 750 ml corked bottles for sale at the pubs.

Russian Imperial Stout
IMPERIAL STOUT **9.5%** ABV
Rich, dark-chocolate aroma with supporting coffee notes. Deep chocolate flavors, balanced by roasty bitterness.

Pig Iron Porter
PORTER **5.4%** ABV
One of their first beers. Roasted and rich, it's a full-flavored blend of coffee, prunes, and dark cherries.

Jacobsen Brewhouse

Gamle Carlsberg Vej 11,
DK-2500 Valby, **DENMARK**
www.jacobsenbeer.com

Named after Carlsberg's founder,
Jacobsen was established in 2005
to produce high-quality specialty
beers with a Scandinavian touch.
This brewhouse will remain in
the original 1847 Carlsberg
brewery complex.

BREWING SECRET Jacobsen also brews
an exclusive Vintage series, matured in
oak barrels.

Jacobsen Saaz Blonde
PALE ALE 7.1% ABV

Extract of angelica adds a juniperlike
flavor that complements the fruity taste of
the yeast.

Jacobsen Extra Pilsner
PILSNER 5.5% ABV

A premium lager using Nordic ingredients
such as Danish organic pilsner malt and
Swedish sea buckthorn juice.

Jämtlands Bryggeri

Box 224, SE-831 23 Östersund,
SWEDEN
www.jamtlandsbryggeri.se

This innovative small microbrewery was established in 1996 in the capital of the Jämtland region of central Sweden. It brews a wide variety of beer, including a strong English ale, Baltic Porter, and Vienna lager. It consistently wins awards at the Stockholm Beer Festival.

BREWING SECRETS It draws from British, German, and Alsace beer styles.

President
PORTER **4.8%** ABV
This bottom-fermented beer has a medium bitterness and the soft aroma of Czech Saaz hops.

Oatmeal Porter
PORTER **4.7%** ABV
An unfiltered and top-fermented porter with a ruby-black color. Espresso in a glass!

Jandelsbrunner

Hauptstr. 17, 94118 Jandelsbrunn,
GERMANY
www.jandelsbrunner.de

The Langs have owned this
brewery since 1810. In the 20th
century, there was renewal of
equipment such as new filling
machines, and the construction
of new production plants and
maturing cellars.

BREWING SECRET In 2004 photovoltaic
equipment was added, to harness the
power of the sun for brewing.

Doppelbock

DOPPELBOCK 8% ABV
The color of this doppelbock is
mahogany, the taste malty, flowery, and
slightly sweet, with a nice bitter note
when finishing.

Ur-Weizen

WHEAT BEER 5.3% ABV
Amber-colored and cloudy from the yeast,
this malty beer tastes flowery with a mild,
sweet finish.

Jennings

Cockermouth, Cumbria,
CA13 9NE **ENGLAND**
www.jenningsbrewery.co.uk

John Jennings had already been brewing for 46 years when he built his own brewery in 1874 in the shadow of Cockermouth Castle. The brewery stands at the confluence of the Cocker and Derwent rivers, and has been owned by Marstons since 2005.

BREWING SECRET Pure Lakeland water is a key ingredient in Jennings ales.

Cumberland Ale
BITTER 4% ABV
Florally hoppy, its intense, full flavor and firm, creamy body slide into a dry aftertaste.

Sneck Lifter
STRONG BITTER 5.1% ABV
Dark and fascinating, with complex aromatics, and generous flavors of fruit and roasted malt.

Jever

Elisabethufer 18, 26441 Jever,
GERMANY
www.jever.de

Jever is one of the top breweries in Germany. Established 160 years ago, the company started producing its export beer in the 1950s. The pilsner as we know it took off during the "pils-wave" of the 1960s. Radeberger bought Jever in 2005.

BREWING SECRET Jever is famous for making one of the driest pilsners in existence.

Jever Fun
LOW ALCOHOL **0.25%** ABV
Almost alcohol-free, but with a similar taste to the pilsner. Hop-bitters and a pilsner taste pervade this golden beer.

Jever Pilsener
PILSNER **4.8%** ABV
The master brewers use a lot of hops at Jever, and their bitterness makes this pilsner very dry.

Jolly Pumpkin

3115 Broad Street
Dexter, MI 48130, **USA**
www.jollypumpkin.com

Not quite like any other brewery
in the US, Jolly Pumpkin Artisan
Ales allows its beers to develop
under the influence of local wild
yeast. All beers are aged in
barrels, and are often blended
and re-fermentated in the bottle
to deliver effervescent beer.
Though its output is small,
the brewery has developed a
national following.

Oro de Calabaza
BELGIAN STRONG GOLDEN ALE 8% ABV
Golden and cloudy, tart and spicy,
with orchard fruit and citrus. Develops
with age.

Bam Biere
SAISON 4.5% ABV
The whole exceeds the sum of its
parts in this "farmhouse" ale, from the
hops (billowing head, dry finish) to the
spicy malts.

Jopen

Minckelersweg 2a,
2031 EM Haarlem, **NETHERLANDS**
www.jopen.nl

Jopen was founded in 1995 with
the intention of recreating old
beer styles specifically from the
Haarlem locale— once an
important brewing center. This is
Holland's only brewery to
concentrate on local recipes, and
no other in the world produces
beer in these styles. A brewpub to
showcase the beers is due to
open soon.

Jopen Koyt
GRUIT BEER 8.5% ABV
A recreation of a pre-hop beer brewed
from three grains and herbs. Fruity, spicy,
and delicious.

Jopen Hoppenbier
AMBER ALE 6.5% ABV
Based on a recipe from 1501 using
barley, wheat, and oats; hints of
coriander, ginger, and cloves complement
spicy hops.

Kelham Island

Sheffield, South Yorkshire,
S3 8SA **ENGLAND**
www.kelhambrewery.co.uk

Since Kelham Island opened in
1990, Sheffield's four large
breweries have closed down,
which makes Kelham's success
all the more remarkable. An
astonishing range of awards has
been collected along the way.

BREWING SECRET Pale Rider and Easy
Rider both make great use of highly
fragrant American hops.

Pale Rider
STRONG BITTER 5.2% ABV
Strong but delicately fruity multi-award
winner, which profits from an
adventurous use of American hops.

Easy Rider
BITTER 4.3% ABV
A subtle pale ale, its initial crisp
bitterness surrendering only to a
lingering fruity palate.

Keo

Franklin Roosevelt Ave, Limassol,
3602 **CYPRUS**
www.keogroup.com

Limassol is the main port and
fastest-growing city on the island
of Cyprus. It is also home to the
Keo Brewery, and no trip to
Limassol is complete without
visiting the plant, which lies just
beyond the Old Port. During
the week, there is a daily tour
around the brewery—finishing,
of course, in the tasting room.

Keo

LAGER 4.5% ABV
A pale lager with a thick head and a sweet
malt taste, it is easy on the palate and
very drinkable.

Five Beer

LAGER 5% ABV
Deep amber in color, it is rich in malt and
low in bitterness. Sweet in the finish.

Klein Duimpje

Parallelweg 2, 2182 CP Hillegom,
NETHERLANDS
www.kleinduimpje.nl

This is the brewery of a prize-winning amateur brewer, Erik Bouman, whose porter was chosen as the best of more than 400 entries at the Dutch Homebrewing Championship of 1997. Bouman's competition success prompted him to start brewing professionally.
His extensive range of top-fermenting ales includes his celebrated porter.

Hillegoms Tarwe Bier
WITBIER 5.5% ABV
Flavored with coriander and orange peel, this wheat beer is spicy, citric, and just ever so slightly sweet.

Porter
PORTER 5.5% ABV
Espressolike roast malt combines with a chocolate sweetness, backed up with liquorice and toast.

Kona

75-5629 Kuakini Highway
Kailua Kona, HI 97640, **USA**
www.konabrewingco.com

Sales are booming everywhere
for Kona Brewing, which offers
mainland drinkers "a pint of
paradise." The Big Island
brewery added capacity to meet
growing demand in Hawaii,
while sales in 17 mainland states
have increased even faster. Beers
sold on the mainland are made
under contract at Widmer
Brothers in Oregon.

Pipeline Porter
PORTER **5.4%** ABV
Brewed with local Kona coffee, its flavor
is well-integrated. Roasty malt, oily, with
chocolate notes.

Fire Rock Pale Ale
PALE ALE **6%** ABV
Reddish-orange with slightly sweet
caramel aromas and flavor, spicy
and citric hops are cleverly integrated
and balanced.

König Ludwig

Augsburger Stre. 41, 82256
Fürstenfeldbruck, **GERMANY**
www.kaltenberg.de

The history of the Bavarian royal
family, the Wittelsbachers, is
closely connected with the art of
beermaking. Today, HRH
Luitpold Prince of Bavaria
continues the family business
successfully with his brands
König Ludwig and Kaltenberg.
The latter brand name refers to
the brewery at Kaltenberg Castle.

König Ludwig Dunkel
DUNKEL 5.1% ABV
Amber, with a smooth taste of dark malt
and fine hops, this is the most popular
dunkel in Germany.

König Ludwig Weissbier
WHEAT BEER 5.5% ABV
One of the most popular wheat beers
in Bavaria; cloudy yellow, with fine hops
in the finish. A very traditional, non-
filtered specialty.

De Koninck

Mechelse Steenweg 291,
B2018 Antwerpen, **BELGIUM**
www.dekoninck.be

De Koninck is an icon—as is its
main beer. It embodies the town
of Antwerp—whose inhabitants
are a proud lot, and will say so.
The amber "bolleke" (actually the
glass) is still the staple diet in
many bars.

BREWING SECRET The draft version
is unpasteurized and should be tried
at its source.

De Koninck

AMBER "SPECIALE BELGE" 5% ABV
Amber malts, residual sugars, and hops
give excellent balance to a fine ale, with a
slight but distinct sulfury aroma and
biscuit character. The draft version
is particularly good—available in cask in
the UK as well.

Krone Tettnang

Bärenplatz 7, 88069 Tettnang,
GERMANY
www.krone-tettnang.de

Krone Tettnang is a small craft
brewery that has been owned by
the Tauscher family for seven
generations. It is a member of
"Brewers with Body and Soul"
—a group of ten small companies
who aim to produce beer "in
another, but traditional, way...."

BREWING SECRET The first organic
beer of the Bodensee region was made
here in 1993.

Keller-Pils
PILSNER 4.7% ABV
The famous first organic beer of the
region. Unfiltered and cloudy, it has the
typical pilsner bitterness of hops and
some sweetness of malt.

Kronenbier
LAGER 4.9% ABV
Richly flavored traditional beer with the
finest possible malt aroma, and
a light finish of fine hops.

Krušovice

270 53 Krušovice 1,
CZECH REPUBLIC
www.pivo-krusovice.cz

When the original owner, Jiří Birka, offered the brewery for sale in 1581 to Emperor Rudolf II, the inventory read: "The brewery kettle is made of stone, so it may be cooked upon immediately." Those documents still exist, but Birka would hardly recognize the highly-mechanized, industrial brewery today—currently the nation's fifth-largest producer.

Krušovice Imperial
PREMIUM LAGER 5.5% ABV
A dry straw aroma heightens a bitter palate, with a floral hop and malt finish.

Krušovice Dark Beer
DARK BEER 3.8% ABV
Roast malt and caramel generosity meet earthy and nutty nuances before a citrus hop finale.

Kuhnhenn

5919 Chicago Road
Warren, MI 48092, **USA**
www.kbrewery.com

Brothers Brett and Eric
Kuhnhenn turned the hardware
store their father ran for 35 years
into a small brewery, winery,
meadery, and brew-on-premises
(where customers can make their
own beer). The national
reputation of Kuhnhenn shows
how word of mouth—and the
Internet—can help small
breweries develop
a cult following.

Raspberry Eisbock

EISBOCK **10.6%** ABV

A small-run beer. Complex, rich with
raspberries, chocolate, warming alcohol,
and a closing tartness.

Penetration Porter

PORTER **5.9%** ABV

Almost black, with roasted coffee,
chocolate, and dark fruits like cherry
filling the nose and the mouth. Citrussy
hop finish.

Kulmbacher

Lichtenfelser Str. 9, 95326
Kulmbach, **GERMANY**
www.kulmbacher.de

The name of Kulmbach, a city in
northern Bavaria, is known to
beer-lovers throughout the world.
Its fame began with the offerings
of beer master Wolfgang Reichel
in 1846. Since his time, many
other brands have joined the
company, and production is now
about 70 million gallons (300
million liters) of beer each year.

Mönchshof Schwarzbier
SCHWARZBIER **4.9**% ABV
Dark roasted malts and fine hops. The
deep, dark color and fine aroma are
typical of schwarzbiers.

Kapuziner Weissbier
WHEAT BEER **5.4**% ABV
Naturally cloudy, sparkling and with a
sweet and fruity taste; this unfiltered beer
is typical of the wheat beer style.

Lagunitas

1280 North McDowell Boulevard
Petaluma, CA 94954, **USA**
www.lagunitas.com

Always known for its hop-driven
beers, Lagunitas launched a new
range in 2006, each one
commemorating a Frank Zappa
album and released
40 years after the album of the
same name. Founder Tony Magee
obtained the permission of the
Zappa Family Trust to use the
original album art on the bottle
label for these beers.

India Pale Ale

INDIA PALE ALE **5.7% ABV**
Brimming with hop character—orange,
grapefruit, peaches, pine—over
malty sweetness.

Kill Ugly Radio

INDIA PALE ALE **7.8% ABV**
Only in the US is this an IPA. Caramel and
fermentation fruit are balanced by spicy,
citrussy, and bitter Northwest hops.

Lakefront

1872 North Commerce Street,
Milwaukee, WI 53212, **USA**
www.lakefrontbrewery.com

Lakefront Brewing, known since
1987 for a range of robust beers,
recently moved to the fore in
brewing New Grist gluten-free
beer for celiacs who cannot
tolerate the grains traditionally
used in making beer.

BREWING SECRET New Grist is brewed
from sorghum, hops, water, rice, and
gluten-free yeast grown on molasses.

New Grist
GLUTEN FREE 5% ABV
A tang of citrus zest to start, then
a light palate with hints of fruit. Mildy
astringent and tart.

Riverwest Stein
VIENNA LAGER 6% ABV
Lightly toasted aromas with hints of
caramel. More caramel in the mouth, and
hop citrus fruitiness. Woody undertones.

Lambrate

Via Adelchi 5, 20131 Milano, **ITALY**
www.birrificiolambrate.com

The first (and still the best) brewpub in Milan, founded in 1996 by brothers Davide and Giampaolo Sangiorgi and their friend Fabio Brocca after a visit to 't IJ Brewery in Amsterdam. They have recently expanded production, adding some new, interesting ales. The menu features some creative beer-influenced dishes, such as pork cooked in beer mash.

Ghisa

SMOKED ALE 5% ABV
Ebony in color with a "cappuccino" foam; lighty smoked, easy to drink, and balanced, with plum notes and a long, hoppy finish.

Montestella

BLOND ALE 4.9% ABV
Their flagship ale; pale, with fresh aromas of hay and hops with a long, dry finish cleansing the palate.

Lao Brewery

Km 12 Thadeua Road,
Vientiane, **LAOS**
www.beer-lao.com

The Lao Brewery began
production in 1973 and was
originally known as Brasseries et
Glaci è res du Laos. Two years
later, in 1975, it became state
owned. In 2002, Carlsberg and
TCC, a Thai company, each
agreed to acquire a 25 percent
stake in Lao Brewery; the
remaining shares are still held
by the Laos government.

Beerlao
LAGER 5% ABV
Described as Asia's best beer, Beerlao has
a pleasant sweetness. Light bitterness,
with hints of honey.

Beerlao Dark
LAGER 6.5% ABV
Reddish brown, it is full of sweet
toffee and toast flavors. A short but
warming finish.

Lees

Manchester, M24 2AX **ENGLAND**
www.jwlees.co.uk

Established by the far-sighted
John Lees in 1878, when
Manchester was becoming the
"workshop of the world," Lees
expanded rapidly, matching the
growing local thirst. Sixth-
generation family members
currently run the brewery and
pub estate, and they remain
faithful to the brewery's maxim:
"We think of ourselves as
old-fashioned and cutting-edge."

Moonraker

BARLEY WINE 7.5% ABV
Powerfully fruity on a rich roast
malt base, with a sweet tendency and
dryish finish.

JW Lees Bitter

BITTER 4% ABV
Classic amber-colored northern bitter,
with layers of malt in the mouthfeel and
a citrus finale.

Lefebvre

54, Rue du Croly,
B1430 Quenast, **BELGIUM**
www.brasserielefebvre.be

The first member of the Lefebvre
family to be involved in brewing
was Jules in 1876. The brewery is
now in the hands of the sixth
generation, with Paul Lefebvre.

BREWING SECRET For a family
brewery, this one is very outward looking,
and now 80 percent of its beer production
is exported.

Floreffe Double
BROWN ABBEY ALE **6.3**% ABV
An ale of a chocolatey kind, which
develops madeira and port notes with
a little ageing.

Saison 1900
SAISON **5.2**% ABV
One of the few that refers to the
brewery's past; delicate farmyard and
rose water aromas.

Left Hand

1265 Boston Avenue
Longmont, CO 80501, **USA**
www.lefthandbrewing.com

The company takes its name from
the Arapahoe Chief Niwot, his
name translating as "left hand."
Originally brewing English-style
ales, the brewery merged in 1998
with Tabernash, known for
Bavarian-inspired beers. Those
beers have now been phased out,
but Left Hand continues to
develop a wide range of beer
styles and produces many
seasonal brews too.

Milk Stout
MILK STOUT 5.3% ABV
Complex and smooth, chocolate and
burnt toast in the aroma and flavor
constantly balanced by creamy sweetness.

Blackjack Porter
PORTER 5.2% ABV
Chocolate and liquorice aromas, medium
body, with hints of dark cherries and a
smooth, dry finish.

Leinenkugel's

1 Jefferson Avenue
Chippewa Falls, WI 54729, **USA**
www.leinie.com

Since 1988, when Miller
Brewing bought a controlling
interest, the Jacob Leinenkugel
Brewing Company has grown
into one of the largest regional
breweries in the country,
distributing in almost
every state.

BREWING SECRET The brewery,
founded in 1867, still offers a range
reflecting its German heritage.

Creamy Dark

US DARK LAGER **4.9%** ABV
As creamy as promised, chocolate with
coffee and cream character and a dryish
not-too-bitter finish.

Sunset Wheat

US WHEAT BEER **4.9%** ABV
Light but complex beer, almost a fruit
salad of aromas and flavors, with some
wheaty tartness and coriander spiciness.

Liefmans

Aalststraat 200,
B9700 Oudenaarde, **BELGIUM**
www.liefmans.be

Although Liefmans parent group
went into receivership at the end
2007, it looks likely that Duvel
Moortgat will take over, and so
the Oudenaarde plant has a good
chance of survival—if, as before,
for lagering purposes only.

BREWING SECRET Liefmans beers are
rare survivors from the once famous
Oudenaards bruin style.

Liefmans Goudenband
OUD BRUIN 8% ABV
A strong interpretation of the style, its
underlying acidity lending the beer
outstanding ageing possibilities.

Liefmans Kriek
OUD BRUIN 6% ABV
The lighter version, refermented with
sour cherries. The rare, un-sweetened
draft version is stellar.

Lindemans

Lenniksebaan 1479, B1602
Vlezenbeek, **BELGIUM**
www.lindemans.be

When considering lambic
breweries, we tend to think about
small farm brewers. Lindemans
may seem to fit this bill at first
glance, yet it is also on the
margins of the 10 largest
breweries in Belgium. Its success
is owed to the rather sweetish
fruit concoctions it excels in,
with nearly half of the produce
destined for foreign markets.

Lindemans Gueuze Cuvée René
GUEUZE 5% ABV
Initially produced on demand for export,
now this caramel-and-sour-apple gueuze
is fairly common.

Lindemans Kriek Cuvée René
KRIEK 5% ABV
Unfiltered kriek is rare and this
bottled beer is a dry notch above the
draft sweet version.

Lion

700 North Pennsylvania Avenue
Wilkes-Barre, PA 18705, **USA**
www.lionbrewery.com

The Lion Brewery, founded in 1905, is a survivor—the last of dozens of breweries that once operated in northeastern Pennsylvania. Most recently the brewery has emphasized this heritage with its Stegmaier brand of good-value traditional beers, the roots of which go back to 1857.

Steg 150
VIENNA LAGER 5.5% ABV
Created to celebrate the brewery's 150th anniversary. Smells like warm toast, malt-accented, lightly sweet but smooth, not cloying.

Stegmaier Porter
PORTER 5.5% ABV
Notes of sweet chocolate and ripe fruit matched with toasty malt and a coffee-bitter finish.

Lion Brewery

254 Colombo Road, Biyagama,
SRI LANKA
www.lionbeer.com

The company's best-known beer
is the bottle conditioned Lion
Stout. The beer is brewed from
British, Czech, and Danish malts,
with Styrian hops and an English
yeast strain. All the ingredients
are transported along precarious
roads to the brewery, located
3,500 ft (1,000 m) above sea level
in the midst of tea plantations.

Lion Stout

STOUT 8% ABV

A world-class beer, with pruney, mocha
aromas and flavors. It has a tarlike
oiliness of body and a peppery, bitter-
chocolate finish. The alcohol gives it a
long warming finish.

Little Creatures

40 Mews Road, Fremantle,
Western Australia 6160,
AUSTRALIA
www.littlecreatures.com.au

Based in an enormous
hangarlike building on the
water's edge at Fremantle, Little
Creatures combines a bar/
restaurant within a busy
microbrewery. The flagship Pale
Ale is inspired by the likes of the
US-based Sierra Nevada, and,
along with the venue, has been a
runaway success. The company is
currently gearing up production,
and has announced bold plans
for themed bars in Sydney and
Melbourne, and a second
brewery to be built in Victoria.

Little Creatures Pale Ale
US PALE ALE **5.2% ABV**
Citrus/grapefruit hop aromatics; chewy
malt and citrus-tinged, robust bitterness.

Rogers' Beer
AMBER ALE **3.8% ABV**
Biscuity malt notes; caramel-laced
mid-palate and spicy-citrus hoppiness;
short finish.

Locher

Industriestrasse 12, CH - 9050
Appenzell, **SWITZERLAND**
www.appenzellerbier.ch

Appenzell is Switzerland's
smallest province (kanton), but
the beer produced by the local
brewery has won it a lot of fame.

BREWING SECRET In the 1990s, the
Locher family found out that beers
brewed on the full moon ferment more
easily; they have, therefore, created a line
of "Vollmond-brews."

Vollmond

ORGANIC LAGER **5.2**% ABV

An aroma of hops and lemon zest;
medium body—chewy; hoppy, but not
excessively bitter.

Holzfass-Bier

LAGER **5.2**% ABV

Aromas of sweetcorn, very little
carbonation, and a distinctive note from
the oak in which it is matured.

Lord Nelson

19 Kent Street, The Rocks, Sydney,
New South Wales 2000, **AUSTRALIA**
www.lordnelsonbrewery.com

Still going strong after 20-plus
years, Sydney's original modern
brewpub attracts ale lovers to
this historic hotel, which
claims to be the city's "oldest
continuously licensed pub." The
early brews were basic malt
extract-based beers, but have
evolved into tasty and complex
ales, worthy of this gem of a
watering hole.

Old Admiral
STRONG ALE **6.1%** ABV
Dense, malty palate, with plummy notes,
lively bitterness, and a warming
afterglow.

Three Sheets
PALE ALE **4.9%** ABV
Malty, fruity aromatics; malt-accented,
with citrus and apricot hints; well-
rounded bitterness.

Lost Abbey

155 Mata Way
San Marcos, CA 92069, **USA**
www.lostabbey.com

Port Brewing, born out of a successful chain of brewpubs in the San Diego area, launched the Lost Abbey brand in 2006, and quickly built up devoted following. Brewmaster Tomme Arthur oversees the ageing room, conjuring up what are best thought of as "Wild American" ales—malt-accented beers enhanced by the barrels in which they are matured.

BREWING SECRET The wooden barrels that once held wines and whiskies now nurture wild yeasts.

Red Poppy
SOUR ALE 5.5% ABV
Brown ale with sour cherries, aged in French oak wine barrels for a year. Oaky, with pleasing acidity.

Judgment Day
BELGIAN STRONG DARK ALE 10.5% ABV
Dark and powerful, with profoundly fruity aromas and palate; chocolate and whisky malt undertones.

Löwenbräu

Nymphenburger Str. 7, 80335
München, **GERMANY**
www.loewenbraeu.de

Löwenbräu is one of the most famous brands in the world. The company is more than 500 years old. In 1948, only three years after the end of World War II, Löwenbräu began exporting again: first to Switzerland, then further afield. In 1997 there was a marriage between Löwenbräu and Spatenbräu; today both are part of the global player InBev.

Löwenbräu Triumphator
DOPPELBOCK 7.6% ABV
Dark brown in color, the Triumphator has a strong flavor of malt, but only a subtle aroma of hops. Sweet.

Löwenbräu Urtyp
EXPORT 5.4% ABV
A balanced flavor with fine aromas of malt; full-bodied, pleasant, and fresh, with mild hops in the finish.

Mad River

195 Taylor Way
Blue Lake, CA 95525, **USA**
www.madriverbrewing.com

Founder Bob Smith built his
brewery in 1989 using recycled
materials, and has since
received many awards for
its waste-reduction programs.
Mad River reuses 98 percent of
its residuals and generates just
one yard/cubic meter of waste a
month while brewing about
250,000 gallons of beer per year.

Jamaica Red Ale

AMBER ALE **6.6%** ABV
First made for the annual reggae festival.
Sweetish nose, with crystal malts and
solid, refreshing hops.

Steelhead Scotch Porter

PORTER **6.4%** ABV
Distinctly a porter, with roasted malt and
a touch of sourness. Caramel notes and
hints of smoke add complexity.

Magic Hat

5 Bartlett Road
Burlington, VT 05403, **USA**
www.magichat.net

Magic Hat's unique and sometimes outrageous packaging and its "non-style" beers have brought double-digit growth year after year. It began in 2008 with construction underway to double capacity, and plans to push distribution into the midwest and south.

BREWING SECRET The Orlio range of beers are certified organic.

#9
PALE ALE 4.6% ABV
Apricot-infused. Subtle stone fruits on the palate, sometimes buttery notes. Finishes dry.

Roxy Rolles
AMBER ALE 5.8% ABV
Brewed for the winter season, rich with caramel and grapefruit aromas and flavors, balanced by closing bitterness.

Maisel

Hindenburgstr. 9, 95445 Bayreuth,
GERMANY
www.maisel.com

Hans and Eberhardt Maisel
founded the brewery in the city
of Richard Wagner in 1887. The
family decided to concentrate
the production on wheat beer
in 1955, and Maisel became a
trendsetter for this style.

BREWING SECRET Their success is the
result of a high level of ability in the
hand-crafting of beers.

Maisel's Weisse
WHEAT BEER 5.2% ABV
The color is typical for Maisel: a
gleaming red. Fermentation in the
bottle gives the beer fruity notes and
mild nuttiness in the finish.

Maisel's Dampfbier
SPECIAL BEER 4.9% ABV
A very old-fashioned beer: the mix of
different malts gives it a really special,
fine character.

Malt Shovel

99 Pyrmont Bridge Road,
Camperdown, Sydney,
New South Wales 2050, **AUSTRALIA**
www.maltshovel.com.au

Positioned as Lion Nathan's craft brewing arm, the Malt Shovel Brewery has an impressive portfolio of beer styles under brewmaster Dr. Charles "Chuck" Hahn. The brewery's first release in 1998 was Amber Ale, which found ready acceptance with traditional lager drinkers. Their James Squire brands are named after a former convict and highwayman, who became the colony's first successful hop grower and brewer.

Malt Shovel India Pale Ale

INDIA PALE ALE **5.6%** ABV

Chewy, caramel-tinged maltiness balanced by robust (dry-hopped) hop flavor and lingering bitterness.

James Squire Porter

PORTER **5%** ABV

Hints of coffee, dark chocolate, and dark fruit (plums); a sumptuous beer, with a smooth finish.

Marston's

Burton upon Trent, Staffordshire,
DE14 2BW **ENGLAND**
www.marstonsbeercompany.co.uk

The company operates three
sites: the Park Brewery in
Wolverhampton, which brews
Banks's, Hanson's, and Mansfield
beers; Jennings Brewery at
Cockermouth in the Lake
District, and the Albion Brewery
in Burton upon Trent.
Throughout its long existence it
has acquired several of
its competitors. Then, in 1999,
Marston's itself was taken over
by Wolverhampton & Dudley
Breweries, which changed its
name to Marston's PLC in 2007.

Pedigree

BEST BITTER 4.4% ABV
A British institution—sweetly hop-laden,
with the vague sulfur aroma that's
characteristic of Burton ales.

Old Empire

INDIA PALE ALE 5.7% ABV
A stylish India Pale Ale, with hop and
fruit flavors and a dry extra-hop finish.

Matilda Bay

130 Stirling Highway, North
Fremantle, Western Australia 6159,
AUSTRALIA
www.matildabay.com.au

Australia's first modern craft
brewery kicked off in Fremantle
in 1984, was acquired by Foster's
six years later, and has been
revitalized in recent times.
Original brews such as Redback
(a hefeweizen) and Dogbolter (a
dark lager) have been
supplemented with a wide range
of beer styles. Much of the new
direction occurred under the
watch of head brewer Brad
Rogers, who has since left the
Foster's fold after 15 years to
embark on a new brewing venture.

Dogbolter
DARK LAGER 5.2% ABV
Roasty, dark chocolate notes; complex
mid-palate; smooth, coffee-ish finish.

Bohemian Pilsner
CZECH PILSNER 5% ABV
A solid maltiness to the pilsner
is well balanced with a generous
hop bitterness.

McAuslan

5080 St-Ambroise, Montréal,
Québec, H4C 2G1, **CANADA**
www.mcauslan.com

McAuslan Brewing began in
January of 1989 when its founder
Peter McAuslan decided to turn
his home-brewing hobby into a
business. It quickly established
itself as one of the area's best
microbreweries and was one
of the first in Canada to bottle
its products. It produces a
challenging range of
seasonal beers.

St-Ambroise Apricot Ale

FRUITY WHEAT BEER 5% ABV
Apricot essence and malted wheat
combine to create an original tasting beer
with a clean, fruit nose.

St-Ambroise Oatmeal Stout

STOUT 5% ABV
Brewed from dark malts and roasted
barley, this stout carries strong espresso
and chocolate notes.

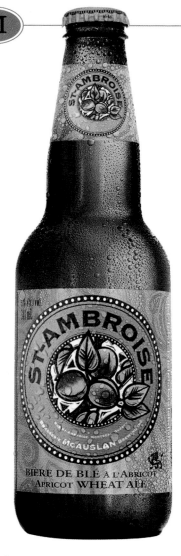

Meantime

Greenwich, London,
SE7 8RX **ENGLAND**
www.meantimebrewing.com

Preferring to be known as the brewery that can't be pigeonholed could be self-regarding, but the approach of master brewer Alastair Hook is purposeful—to demonstrate the exciting flavor potential that beer has to offer.

BREWING SECRET Research into, and recreation of, beers from the past is an abiding passion here, as exemplified by Meantime's India Pale Ale.

Meantime Chocolate
SPECIALITY STRONG BEER **6.5% ABV**
Complex malt structure, with dark chocolate releasing vanilla notes to create a rich, memorable infusion.

India Pale Ale
INDIA PALE ALE **7.5% ABV**
Massively hoppy, with herbal, spice, and grass tiers grasping the strength of the original IPAs.

Mendocino

South Highway 101
Hopland, CA 13351, **USA**
www.mendobrew.com

Mendocino Brewing was one of
the first success stories among
US "boutique" breweries (as they
were called at the time). It
opened in 1983 as the Hopland
Brewery, having acquired
equipment, the house yeast, and
even a few employees from the
groundbreaking, but by then
defunct, New Albion Brewery.

Red Tail Ale
AMBER ALE **6.1%** ABV
An earthy nose includes hints of
orchard fruits. Layers of creamy malt
with notes of liquorice.

Blue Heron
PALE ALE **6.1%** ABV
Orange zest and lemon rind to start,
giving way to traditional biscuity malt
and a balanced, moderate bitterness.

Mettlacher Abteibräu

Bahnhofstr. 32, 66693 Mettlach,
GERMANY
www.abtei-brauerei.de

Mettlacher specializes in natural, unfiltered beer. Guests can watch the brewing process from the attached restaurant. The brewers promote the beer styles of the region and run courses on beer production.

BREWING SECRET High-quality basic products, modern techniques, and the energy of the brewers ensure success.

Abtei-Bock
BOCK **6.2%** ABV
Strong-roasted bock with obvious roasty aromas and an even more intense flavor of fine hops.

Abtei-Josef-Sud
WHEAT BEER **5.1%** ABV
The dark amber-colored wheat beer is sparkling and has typical aromas from the mash of wheat and barley malts.

Michigan

1093 Highview Drive
Webberville, MI 48892, **USA**
www.michiganbrewing.com

Although Michigan Brewing was one of the state's biggest breweries before it bought the defunct Celis brand from international giant Miller, it is now best known for that range of beers. Belgian in style, they were first created by Pierre Celis (brewer of the original Hoegaarden beer) after he moved to Texas. Celis even helped brew the first batches made in Michigan.

Celis White
WITBIER **4.25**% ABV
Cloudy, coriander-spicy, with citrus all the way through, wheat tartness, and a soft finish.

Mackinac Pale Ale
PALE ALE **5.5**% ABV
The brewery flagship, golden-orange, not quite pale, with substantial malt fruitiness. Earthy and citrussy American hops.

Mikkeller

Slien 2, 2.tv,
DK-1766 Copenhagen, **DENMARK**
www.mikkeller.dk

An innovative brewery producing an eclectic range of beer. Mikkeller adopts an American rule-breaking approach to brewing and has achieved significant international recognition with several of its brews.

BREWING SECRET The brewery recently introduced Black, the strongest beer ever made by a Danish brewer.

Beer Geek Breakfast
OATMEAL STOUT 7.5% ABV
An award-winning stout with a rich nose, smooth and balanced taste, and coffee and chocolate notes.

Black
IMPERIAL STOUT 17.5% ABV
Exceptional body of sugars, roasted coffee beans, and black chocolate; a complex and lingering aftertaste.

Minhas

1208 14th Avenue
Monroe, WI 53566, **USA**
www.minhasbrewery.com

Ravinder Minhas was just 24
years old when he bought the
historic Joseph Huber Brewery
in 2006 to produce his popular
Mountain Creek brands, already
brewed under contract in Monroe
for Canadian distribution.
Minhas Craft Brewery still makes
the Huber brands (dating back to
1843), Berghoff beers, and a line
of grocery store house label
beers as well.

Lazy Mutt
GOLDEN ALE 4.8% ABV
The first released under the Minhas
brand, billed as a "farmhouse ale" by
the brewery but more summer ale than
a *saison*.

Huber Bock
BOCK 5.4% ABV
Toasty and dry, with caramel notes. Best
at Baumgartner's Cheese Store & Tavern
near the brewery.

Minoh AJI

3-19-11 Makiochi, Minoh City,
Osaka 562-0004, **JAPAN**
www.minoh-beer.jp

Established by liquor store owner Masaji Oshita, and run by his daughters Kaori and Mayuko, Minoh AJI brewery mostly makes beers based on American craft beer styles.

BREWING SECRET Among the more distinctive beers are two that contain hemp and one that uses Cabernet Sauvignon grape juice.

Minoh AJI Stout
STOUT 5.5% ABV
Brewed in the Irish style, with lots of roast flavor and creamy texture, this stout has a subdued bitterness.

Double IPA
STRONG IPA 9% ABV
Bold and exciting, this strong beer is only produced as a seasonal so far, but its popularity may lead to it becoming available year-round.

Moa

Jacksons Rd, RD3 Blenheim,
NEW ZEALAND
www.moabeer.co.nz

Nestled among vines in Marlborough's wine country is Moa's brewery and tasting room—the brainchild of winemaker Josh Scott, who wanted to make super premium beers with the winemaking techniques used for Champagne-style sparkling wines.

BREWING SECRET Moa's larger 750 ml bottles undergo the full *méthode traditionelle* production regime.

Moa Original
BOTTLE-CONDITIONED PILS 5.5% ABV
Extended yeast contact rewards this delightful dry, crisp pilsner with a savory toastiness.

Moa Blanc
BOTTLE-CONDITIONED
WHEAT BEER 5.5% ABV
Dry, crisp, hints of banana and vanilla; soft natural carbonation.

Moctezuma

Monterrey/Veracruz-Llave, **MEXICO**
www.femsa.com

Mexico's most innovative brewer, Moctezuma also has operations in Brazil and is an important exporter of beer to the US. It has a powerful brand portfolio that includes Tecate, Dos Equis, Sol, Indio, Bohemia, and Carta Blanc, many of which are sold in style bars worldwide. Its beers tend to be smooth, with a spritzy finish.

Dos Equis

VIENNA LAGER **4.8%** ABV
Rich and dark red, with chocolate orange flavors; its warming sweetness gives way to a long finish.

SOL

LAGER **4.5%** ABV
A crisp, light-bodied lager with a corn syrup aroma.

De Molen

Overtocht 43, 2411 BS Bodegraven,
NETHERLANDS
www.brouwerijdemolen.nl

Since starting Molen in 2004,
brewer Menno Olivier has
quickly gained an enviable
reputation. This is one of only a
handful of Dutch micros to
export; its cask-conditioned beer,
Engel, is designed especially for
the UK market.

BREWING SECRET Aficionados regard
Tsarina Esra, an Imperial porter, as one
of Europe's very finest beers.

Borefts Blond
BLOND ALE **6.5% ABV**
Unlike many blondes, hops dominate
here. Orange, pine, resin, and grass
flavors fill the mouth.

Borefts Stout
STOUT **7% ABV**
Packed with all the roasty malt flavors
you expect from a stout. Complex,
characterful, harmonious.

Biervision Monstein

Monstein, CH-7278 Davos,
SWITZERLAND
www.biervision-monstein.ch

Andreas Aegerter and Christian
Ochs started this village brewery
high up in the mountains near
Davos in 2001, along with 756
small investors (each of them a
devoted customer). They
all shared the vision that there
is a market for unusual beers, as
well as beer-related products,
such as cheese crusted with malt
and spirits distilled from beer.

Mungga
KÖLSCH 3.5% ABV
Brewed from organic Swiss
ingredients, Mungga ("groundhog")
has aromas of violets, a dry taste, and
an elegant bitterness.

Royal 11
SPICED BEER 6.5% ABV
Reddish, with pleasant cherry aromas
(from the local liqueur Röteli); fruity and
only faintly bitter.

Moo Brew

655 Main Road, Berriedale, Hobart,
Tasmania 7011, **AUSTRALIA**
www.moobrew.com.au

A stunningly appointed
microbrewery, with commanding
views of Derwent River and
Mount Wellington from the
second-story, glass-fronted
brewhouse. An off-shoot of
Moorilla Estate winery, Moo
Brew has set a new benchmark
among Australian craft
producers, with slick packaging,
uncompromising beers, and
premium pricing.

Moo Brew Pilsner
CZECH PILSNER 5% ABV
Bright, golden, with finely-beaded
bubbles; honey-ish malt character
balanced by herbal hop bitterness.

Moo Brew Pale Ale
US PALE ALE 4.9% ABV
Citrus aromatics; grapefruit notes
dominate mid-palate, rounded out with
substantial, tingling bitter finish.

Moorhouse's

Burnley, Lancashire,
BB11 5EN **ENGLAND**
www.moorhouses.co.uk

Mineral water and low-alcohol "hop bitters" were William Moorhouse's forte. He started his business in 1865, but his successors failed to achieve a great deal in terms of brewing beer until fresh investment in infrastructure arrived in 1988. Further improvements and additions accelerated growth and helped create the admirable reputation that Moorhouse ales have today.

Pendle Witches Brew

STRONG BITTER **5.1%** ABV
Distinctive and amber-colored,
the beer has a full malty palate and a
resonant fruity hop finale.

Black Cat

MILD **3.4%** ABV
Full, dark, and complex, with distinctive chocolate malt and liquorice flavors, and a hoppy finish.

Moosehead

89 Main Street West, Saint John,
New Brunswick, E2M 3H2, **CANADA**
www.moosehead.ca

Canada's oldest independent
brewery can trace its roots back
to 1867, when Susannah Oland
first started brewing in her
Dartmouth, Nova Scotia
backyard. Today, the company
is still owned and operated by
the Oland family. Moosehead
has stakes in McAuslan and
wholly owns the Niagara Falls
Brewing Company.

Moosehead Lager

LAGER 5% ABV
Pale, staw-colored, clean-tasting session
beer; best drunk cold.

Clancy Amber Ale

ALE 5% ABV
Top-fermented, Clancy's is a reddish
beer, with a distinct malt aroma and
overlays of caramel.

Multi Bintang

Surabaya, Central Java, **INDONESIA**
www.multibintang.co.id

Indonesia's largest brewery
produces and markets a range
of drinks, including Bir Bintang,
Heineken, Guinness Stout, and
the low alcohol Green Sands. It
was founded in 1929, with
Heineken taking a share of the
company in the 1930s. Though
taken over by the Indonesian
government in 1957, Heineken
became involved again in 1967,
and today it is largely owned
by them.

Bintang Bir Pilsener
LAGER 4.8% ABV
A fresh malty aroma gives way to
a dry hoppy bitter finish—the beer clearly
draws on its Dutch ancestry.

Bintang Gold
LAGER 4.8% ABV
A slightly darker variation of the pilsener,
brewed to commemorate the republic's
golden anniversary.

New Belgium

500 Linden Street
Fort Collins, CO 80524, **USA**
www.newbelgium.com

Jeff Lebesch and Kim Jordan
started out with a system, built to
Belgian specifications, in their
cellar in 1991. They now operate
the third largest craft brewery in
the US. Best known for Fat Tire
Ale, the brewery offers quite a
wide range of beers, including its
outstanding Blue Paddle
Pilsener.

BREWING SECRET New Belgium has
more capacity for ageing beer on wood
than any brewery other than Rodenbach
Brewery in Belgium.

Fat Tire
AMBER ALE 5.3% ABV
Biscuity, malty nose, with toasted caramel
in the middle and a balanced finish on the
sweet side of dry.

Mothership Wit
WITBIER 4.8% ABV
The brewery's first organic beer. Fruity
and spicy; a creamy texture and wheat
tartness on the tongue. Refreshing acidity
at the finish.

New Glarus

Highway 69
New Glarus, WI 53574, **USA**
www.newglarusbrewing.com

In 2008, New Glarus Brewing moved into a $21 million plant, just outside a picturesque village settled by Swiss pioneers in 1845. The attractive complex is designed to look like a Wisconsin dairy farm. In 2002 it was a microbrewery that made 13,700 barrels; by 2007, it had increased this fivefold. The expansion allowed the brewery to double production and keep pace with soaring sales and the demand for brewmaster Dan Carey's fruit beers and limited-edition "Unplugged" brews.

Spotted Cow

CREAM ALE **4.8% ABV**
Faintly fruity, tasting of fresh peaches. Pleasantly grainy, light on the tongue, and refreshing.

Fat Squirrel

BROWN ALE **5.5%**
Hazelnuts on the nose, blending with chocolate and caramel flavors; nicely balanced by earthy hops.

New Holland

690 Commerce Court
Holland, MI 49423, **USA**
www.newhollandbrew.com

New Holland Brewing bottle
caps carry the slogan "Art in
Fermented Form," which
extends from beer to a line of
brandy-flavored vodka, gin,
rum, and other spirits. To keep
up with demand for its assertive
beers, the brewery recently put
on line a used copper-domed,
three-vessel brewhouse acquired
from Germany.

The Poet

OATMEAL STOUT 6.5% ABV

Abundant roast, chocolate, and dark,
rummy fruits. Full-bodied and creamy
enough to balance the coffee start.

Black Tulip

TRIPLE 9% ABV

Floral, with candy and honey sweetness,
and fruity notes. Sweet but tart in the
mouth, accented by spicy, bitter hops.

Nils Oscar

Fruängsgatan 2,
SE-611 31 Nyköping, **SWEDEN**
www.nilsoscar.se

This microbrewery and distillery was established in 1996 and makes well-balanced beers that go well with food. It has won many awards, including four medals in the World Beer Cup.

BREWING SECRET Nils Oscar has its own maltings, and a farm where barley and other cereals for malting are grown.

Imperial Stout
IMPERIAL STOUT 7% ABV
Well balanced and rich from ageing. Chocolate aromas with caramel giving way to a bittersweet finish.

India Ale
INDIA PALE ALE 5.3% ABV
Heavily hopped with Amarillo, giving an aroma of tropical fruits; the fruitiness is balanced by the crystal malt sweetness.

Nøgne Ø

Gamle Rykene Kraftstasjon,
Lunde N-4885 Grimstad, **NORWAY**
www.nogne-o.com

Kjetil Jikiun launched Nøgne Ø
("naked island") in 2003 after
learning home-brewing in the
US. Now his brewery is Norway's
largest supplier of bottle-
conditioned ale.

BREWING SECRET Nøgne mixes British
Marris Otter malt with American
C-hops, including Cascade, Centenneal,
Chinook, and Columbus.

Saison
SAISON **6.5%** ABV
East Kent Goldings and Crystal hops and
Belgian ale yeast produce a light and
refreshing brew, available all year but
ideal in summer.

Imperial Stout
IMPERIAL STOUT **9%** ABV
A dark, rich ale with a generous
sweetness and bitterness coming from
the roasted malts.

North Coast

455 North Main Street
Fort Bragg, CA 95437, **USA**
www.northcoastbrewing.com

Since opening in 1988, North
Coast Brewing has cast a larger
shadow than its production levels
would suggest. Though small, it
sells beer in 36 states and exports
to Europe and the Pacific Rim too.
Brewmaster Mark Ruedrich has
further extended North Coast's
reputation by exploring beer
styles before many others. Part of
the profits from one, Brother
Thelonious, go to the Thelonious
Monk Institute of Jazz, earning the
brewery entry into many jazz clubs.

Old Rasputin

IMPERIAL STOUT 11.6% ABV
Powerful, but subtle enough for flavors to
emerge—bitter and sweet chocolate,
burnt barley, rum, toffee, dried dark
fruits, and espresso.

Brother Thelonious

BELGIAN STRONG DARK ALE 9.3% ABV
Spicy and candy-sweet aromas, with dark
fruits, notes of banana and caramelized
sugar, almost rummy.

Oakham

Peterborough, Cambridgeshire,
PE2 7JB **ENGLAND**
www.oakhamales.com

Impressive growth from modest
homebrew origins has led to the
brewery now occupying its third
site since 1993. The original
owner sold the business on in
1995 but the early vision and
ambitions prevail.

BREWING SECRET American hop
varieties, with powerful floral
characteristics, are a feature of the range.

Jeffrey Hudson Bitter / JHB
BITTER 3.8% ABV
Dominant citrus fruit hop aroma, which
continues on the palate, blending into
luscious malt flavors.

White Dwarf
WHEAT BEER 4.3% ABV
An English-style wheat beer, with
flinty bitterness that mellows and
reveals fruit nuances.

Ochakovo

44, Riabinivaya, Moscow, **RUSSIA**
www.ochakovo.ru

Ochakovo is the last independent Russian brewery, and is trying to remain so. Its original brewhouse has been transformed into a museum, which takes visitors, step-by-step, through the brewing process and features many exhibits from the 19th century.

BREWING SECRET In 2005, Ochakovo launched an unpasteurized, unfiltered "live" beer, aimed at the health market.

Ochakovo Classic
LAGER 5% ABV
Corn-yellow in color, with intense malt overtones and a hoppy finish.

Ochakovo Ruby
VIENNA LAGER 3.9% ABV
Pale ruby in color, with aromas of winter fruits and floral notes, it has strong hints of caramel on the palate.

Okell's

Douglas, Isle of Man,
IM2 1QG **ENGLAND**
www.okells.co.uk

Dr. William Okell's steam-powered brewery—which he designed himself in 1874—was regarded as one of the most sophisticated in the world at the time. Okell's new plant, which it moved to in 1994, is the modern equivalent. It is controlled by computers rather than steam, but the passion and commitment to quality beer production remains unaltered.

Doctor Okell's IPA

INDIA PALE ALE **4.4**% ABV
Potential sweetness, offset by a high hopping regime for overall roundness, spiced by lemon notes.

Okell's Bitter

BITTER **3.7**% ABV
Light colored and complexly flavored, with hints of honey and a long-lingering dry finish.

Ommegang

656 County Highway 33
Cooperstown, NY 13326, **USA**
www.ommegang.com

Owned by Belgium's Duvel
Moortgat, Brewery Ommegang
has brewed ales in the Belgian
tradition since 1997, selling
limited quantities across much of
the US. It hosts one of the
nation's most outstanding beer
festivals, Belgium Comes to
Coopers-town, each summer in
the picturesque brewery grounds
outside of town.

Hennepin
SAISON 7.7% ABV
Spicy and peppery throughout. Yeasty
notes, citrus more apparent on the palate.
Tart and dry.

Ommegang Abbey Ale
BELGIAN STRONG DARK ALE 8.5% ABV
The flagship ale, produced in the
spirit of a Christmas beer. Rich and
chocolatey, with underlying liquorice
and festive spices.

Orkney

Stromness, Orkney,
KW16 3LT **SCOTLAND**
www.orkneybrewery.co.uk

Commendable ecological
awareness allows the brewery's
waste water to be filtered through
two neighboring lochs that
support fish and waterfowl. It was
first set up in 1988, and then
thoroughly modernized in 1994.
In 2008, the brewery expanded,
adding a visitor center and shop.
Its output was also increased.

Dark Island
STRONG BITTER **4.6%** ABV
Ruby-red and mysterious, with
blackcurrant fruit on the nose and
a full-roasted malt palate.

Skullsplitter
BARLEY WINE **8.5%** ABV
Forcefully malty nose; hints of
apple, spicy hop, and some nut in the
complex flavorings.

Orval

2, Abbaye de Notre-Dame d'Orval,
B6823 Villers devant Orval,
BELGIUM
www.orval.be

The single Orval Trappist ale is a
symbol of the whole abbey: the
best in early 20th-century Art
Nouveau styling, blending with
the medieval ruins that surround
it. The bottle, glassware, and
everything else is designed with
an eye for beauty and peace. The
ruins can be visited, but alas, not
the newly revamped brewery.

Orval

AMBER ALE **6.2%** ABV

An ultra dry ale that owes a large part of
its character to *Brettanomyces* yeasts,
(not unlike those that define lambic) and
to a high proportion of dry hops.

Ostravar

Hornopolní 57, 728 25 Ostrava 1,
CZECH REPUBLIC
www.ostravar.cz

The Czech Republic's third-largest city lies closer to Katowice in Poland and Vienna in Austria than to Prague, and so prides itself on being "different" to other Czech breweries. Ostravar beers reflect this strategic position, and are carefully considered with local tradition in mind. It has, however, been internationally owned (now by InBev) since 2000.

Ostravar Premium
PREMIUM LAGER **5.1%** ABV
A rich head promoting malt and hop aromas straddle a full-bodied strong bitter bite.

Ostravar Kelt
STOUT **4.8%** ABV
Irish-style stout; pronounced hop and roasted barley aromas which continue throughout the palate.

Otter Creek

793 Exchange Street
Middlebury, VT 05753, **USA**
www.ottercreekbrewing.com

The Wolaver family bought the well-established Otter Creek Brewery in 2002 in order to make its own organic ales, which had previously been made under contract at other breweries. Otter Creek beers are still produced as well, and the "World Tour" series includes Otter Mon (a Jamaican-style stout) and Otteroo (an Australian-style lager).

Otter Creek Copper Ale
ALTBIER 5.4% ABV
Rich, complex, malty aromas and flavors, with a sneaky bitterness that extends the finish.

Wolaver's Oatmeal Stout
OATMEAL STOUT 5.9% ABV
Chocolate and roasted coffee at the outset, blending with creamy notes in the mouth. Full-bodied, but finishing rather dry.

Palmer's

Bridport, Dorset,
DT6 4JA **ENGLAND**
www.palmersbrewery.com

Palmer's is able to claim
continuous production on its
original site over a period of
more than 200 years. From the
outside it has altered little, but
this is a contemporary brewing
operation, offering a diverse
range of ales.

BREWING SECRET Maris Otter malted
barley and Golding hops combine to give
these beers their fruitiness.

Traditional Best Bitter
BEST BITTER **4.2%** ABV
Styled on an India Pale Ale; deliciously
hoppy, with fruit and malt undercurrents.

Tally Ho!
STRONG BITTER **5.5%** ABV
Distinctly nutty and dark, with full-bodied
complexity emerging slowly, then on to a
lingering afterglow.

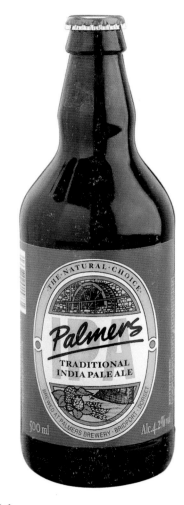

Panil (Torrechiara)

Strada Pilastro 35/a,
43010 Torrechiara (PR), **ITALY**
www.panilbeer.com

Renzo Losi, a biology graduate,
got his brewing break in 2000,
when his winemaker father gave
him permission to make beer at
the family's vineyard estate,
south of Parma.

BREWING SECRET The links with
the family winemaking tradition are
retained in the use of oak barrels and
spumante yeasts.

Panil Barriquée Sour
FLEMISH SOUR RED 8% ABV
The flagship ale, barrel-aged for
three months. Sour, vinous,
and uncompromising.

Divina
WILD BEER 5.5% ABV
Spontaneously fermented by being
left, uncovered, on the back of a truck
in a field overnight. Sweet-sour, yeasty,
and citrussy.

Pelican

33180 Cape Kiwanda Drive
Pacific City, OR 97135, **USA**
www.pelicanbrewery.com

Set on the ocean shore,
Pelican lies just south of Cape
Kiwanda, one of Oregon's most
photographed landmarks. Only
small quantities are sold outside
the pub.

BREWING SECRET Its India Pelican
Ale and Doryman's Dark have both been
named Grand Champion Beer at the
Australian International Beer Awards.

Doryman's Dark Ale
BROWN ALE 5.8% ABV
Malt qualities—roasted nuts, cocoa,
coffee beans, caramel—balanced by
Northwest hops.

Tsunami Stout
STOUT 7% ABV
Deep black, with a creamy head. Coffee
and chocolate on the nose and palate,
rich and almost creamy. Pleasant acidic
bite at the end.

Pete's

14800 San Pedro Avenue
San Antonio, TX 78232, **USA**
www.petes.com

Pete's Brewing was once among
the leading new wave of
American beer companies.
Founder Pete Slosburg sold the
business to San Antonio-based
Gambrinus in 1988, and the
brand has not matched the
success of other Gambrinus
companies. Brewed under
contract in New York, Pete's is
less widely available today.

Pete's Wicked Ale
BROWN ALE 5.3% ABV
The defining American Brown Ale when
brewed to Slosberg's original homebrew
recipe lost its bite when the hopping rate
was halved.

Wicked Strawberry Blond
FRUIT ALE 5% ABV
More blonde than strawberry, but berry
sweetness begins on the nose and
continues through the finish.

Piccolo Birrificio

Via iv Novembre 20,
18035 Apricale (IM), **ITALY**
www.piccolobirrificio.com

This microbrewery, founded in
2005, is housed in a former
olive-oil mill in the lovely
medieval village of Apricale,
near the French border. Brewer
Lorenzo Bottoni produces a
range of fine ales under the
brand name of Nüa ("naked"),
including some amazing
brews using unusual local
fruits and plants.

Sesonette
BELGIAN SAISON 6.5% ABV
Matured in Chardonnay barrels with
spices and local chinotto peel (from a
small, bitter citrus fruit).

Chiostro
SPICED ALE 5% ABV
Spiced with *Artemisia absinthium*
(wormwood), then fermented with
Trappist yeasts, giving complex and
unique aromas and flavors.

Pietra

Route de la Marana,
20600 Furiani, **FRANCE**
www.brasseriepietra.com

The first Corsican brewery
in history opened in 1996.
Brewers Armelle and Dominique
Sialelli use raw materials native
to the island, such as *maquis*
herbs and chestnut flour, which
forms an ingredient rather than
just a flavoring in their Pietra
beer. *Biera Corsa* has been a
great success, both in Corsica
and overseas.

Colomba
WHEAT BEER 5% ABV
Very fresh and sharp, with unusual
aromas of arbutus, myrtle, and juniper.
A refreshing summer beer.

Pietra
AMBER LAGER 6% ABV
Elegant flavors of toasted malts,
nuttiness, and a slight bitterness.

Pilsner Urquell

U Prazdroje 7, 304 97 Plzeň,
CZECH REPUBLIC
www.pilsner-urquell.cz

The Czechs have blessed us with the microwave oven, soft contact lenses, and beer that changed the world. It was, however, a Bavarian who was the key player in the Pilsner Urquell story. As a young brewer, Josef Groll presented the nation with its first pilsner on October 4, 1842. This sensational clear golden beer spread across Europe like wildfire from its "original source."

Pilsner Urquell

CLASSIC PILSNER **4.4%** ABV
The ideal one-and-a-half inch (35 mm) tight head leaves a lacing down the glass with every sip of spiced leaf and preserved fruit flavors, developing a sweet malt piquancy and long, enveloping finish.

PRAGUE, CZECH REPUBLIC

The city of Prague is one of the world's greatest beer destinations. And where better to start a beer trail than in the Old Town Square (Staroměstské náměstí), location of the famous 15th-century Astronomical Clock—one of the world's oldest clocks still in working order. Many bars edge the square, each spilling out on to the cobbles with seating and canopies.

2 U ZLATÉHO TYGRA

One of the Old Town's most atmospheric and oldest bars, U Zlatého Tygra is crowded with small tables, which always seem to be full with locals deep in energetic conversations—so be prepared to stand. It's a favorite of the writer and former Czech President Václav Havel, and President Clinton has also drunk here. The unfiltered Pilsner Urquell is said to be the best in Prague. *Husova 17, Prague*

3 U PINKASŮ

In 1843 U Pinkasů was the first bar in Prague to serve Pilsner Urquell, and it is still available today. The bar was saved from extinction in 2000, when it was extensively refurbished. A more recent refurbishment has opened up more of the building. *Jungmannovo nám, 16/15, Prague*

1 OLD TOWN SQUARE

Here it is possible to sit outside and savor a beer, while watching the thousands of visitors who now flock to the Czech capital. Displays of folk dancing and music can often be enjoyed here too.

NOVOMĚSTSKÝ PIVOVAR

An Art Deco-style entrance leads visitors down an alleyway of shops to this wood-paneled brewery, pub, and restaurant. Unfiltered light and dark beers are available. The food is unashamedly Czech, with specialties such a goulash, tripe soup, and roast knuckle of pork. *Vodickova 20, Prague*

PIVODUM

The Pivodum restaurant and bar is dominated by gleaming coppers. Traditional Czech beers are served, as well as other interesting brews, including a sour cherry beer, a coffee beer, and Samp—a beer champagne. Groups can order eight beers for the price of seven, and they are served in a large giraffelike container. A sample tray of eight beers is available too. *Ječná/Lípová 15, Prague*

U FLEKŮ

Crowded it may be, a haunt of many tourists it certainly is, but U Fleků should not be missed. Brewing began here in 1499, and it is said to be the world's oldest brewpub. It comprises many large rooms, including one for a booming oompah band. It has a small museum and daily brewery tours. The superb house beer is Flekovsky tmavy lezáck, which comes in dark and light versions. *Kremencova 11, Prague*

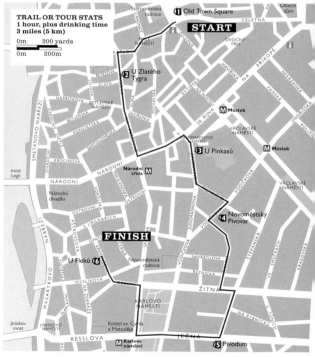

TRAIL OR TOUR STATS
1 hour, plus drinking time
3 miles (5 km)

0m   200 yards
0m   200m

START

FINISH

De Prael

Helicopterstraat 13-15, 1059 CE
Amsterdam, **NETHERLANDS**
www.deprael.nl

Set up with the help of
government grants, Amsterdam's
smallest brewery has a workforce
made up of recovering
psychiatric patients. The first
choice of name—De Parel ("The
Pearl")—had to be changed when
Budels complained that it
infringed on the copyright
of their Parel beer. The solution
was simply to shuffle the letters
of the name around.

Heintje
WITBIER 5.4% ABV
Unspiced, but with prominent citrus
aromas, a touch of fruit, and an
unexpectedly hoppy finish.

Mary
BARLEY WINE 9.6% ABV
Neither malt nor hops dominate this
fruity strong ale, laced with pepper, toffee,
and caramel.

Quilmes

Tte. Gral. Juan D. Peron 667 103,
Buenos Aires, **ARGENTINA**
www.quilmes.com.ar

The dominant beer in Argentina,
Quilmes is now part of the InBev
embrace. Like many breweries in
South America, it was begun by a
German, the brewery and malt
plant being founded in the 1880s
by Otto Bemberg. "Quilmes"
derives from an indigenous name
for the place where the brewery
is located.

Quilmes Cristal
LAGER **4.9%** ABV
Thin and pale, with no aromatic
distractions. Surprisingly drinkable,
though, with refreshing sweetness.

Quilmes Stout
STOUT **4.8%** ABV
Three malts clamor for attention—but the
expected coffee flavors are overwhelmed
by sweetness.

Radegast

739 51 Nošovice, **CZECH REPUBLIC**
www.radegast.cz

Radegast, roughly meaning "dear guest," was the Slavic god of fertility and crops, and consequently became proclaimed god of hospitality too. Despite its nominal connections with the dawn of time, the brewery actually began operating only in 1970. It continues to be one of the country's most technologically advanced and best equipped beer producers.

Radegast Original
PILSNER 4% ABV
A light malt and spiced hop nose, malt-sweet flavors and a crisp, grainy bitterness.

Radegast Premium
PREMIUM LAGER 5% ABV
A characteristic herbal hoppy aroma and medium-sweet malt intensity dwell on cereal notes.

Refsvindinge Brewery

Nyborgvej 80,
DK-5853 Ørbæk, **DENMARK**
www.bryggerietrefsvindinge.dk

Since 1885, four generations
have run this farmhouse
brewery. It was among the first to
brew ales in Denmark and is
credited with developing Danish
white beer *(hvidtøl)* and the
old-style smoked "ship's beer"
(skibsøl), as well as two varieties
of beer for children (not entirely
alcohol free!).

Ale No.16
BROWN ALE 5.7% ABV
Well rounded, typical dark ale using
original English yeast to produce a sweet,
fresh taste.

Mors Stout
PORTER 5.7% ABV
Dark, smooth porter brewed using malt
that has been roasted with cocoa beans.

Ridna Marka

71 Mikgorod str.Radomyshl,
UKRAINE
www.etalon-beer.com.ua/en

Beermaking in Radomyshl dates from 1886, when this brewery was founded by the Czech Albrechtam brothers. They found that the soft water here was ideal for brewing. The modern brewery has adapted Bavarian technology to Ukrainian ingredients.

BREWING SECRET The brewhouse has been specifically designed to produce unfiltered, genuine wheat beers.

Etalon Weissbier
WHEAT BEER 5% ABV
Spicy with a rich, creamy malt note and a long, quenching flavor and finish. Hints of bananas and vanilla.

Robinson's

Stockport, Cheshire,
SK1 1JJ **ENGLAND**
www.frederic.robinson.co.uk

One of the British Isles'
largest regional breweries,
Robinson's began as the Union
Inn in 1838. Sixth-generation
family members are still in
charge of its development,
overseeing huge advances in
brewing and bottling techniques.

BREWING SECRET Tradition continues
here, and the brewery still uses its
surviving 1920s yeast strain.

Old Tom Strong Ale
BARLEY WINE **8.5% ABV**
Full-bodied with an aroma and flavor
alliance of malt, chocolate, fruit, and
port wine.

Unicorn Best Bitter
BEST BITTER **4.2% ABV**
Golden, with some spicy hop and
malt on the nose, countered by a
bittersweet release.

Rochefort

8, Abbaye de Notre Dame de St-Remy,
B5580 Rochefort, **BELGIUM**
www.trappistes-rochefort.com

Though brewing has been carried
out here since 1900, it is only
since 1998 that Rochefort has
used labels on their bottled beer.
Recently, this smallest of the
Walloon Trappist breweries
decided to employ a lay
brewmaster, Gumer Santos, to
work on their beer production.
Since then, an amazing new
lagering room has begun taking
shape next to the abbey church,
and the few visitors allowed into
the abbey are now proudly shown
the new tasting room.

Rochefort 6 (red)
ABBEY ALE 7.5% ABV
Six is a veiled reference to the beer's
density (1060 OG)—and this lightest and
rarest Rochefort enjoys a very fruity taste.

Rochefort 10 (blue)
ABBEY ALE 11.3% ABV
A superior Trappist ale, with toffee,
chocolate, raisins, and port flavors, and
incomparable complexity.

Rodenbach

Spanjestraat 133-141,
B8800 Roeselare, **BELGIUM**
www.rodenbach.be

The Rodenbach family started
making beer in Roeselare in
1821. Now under the wing of
Palm breweries, Rodenbach has
turned resolutely modern, yet
without doing away with its
age-old traditions.

BREWING SECRET The "cathedral" of
wooden fermenters is one of the most
impressive sights in Belgian brewing.

Rodenbach Classic
OUD BRUIN **5%** ABV
Bearing the signs of its mixed
fermentation and wood ageing, it is
vinous in character and refreshing.

Rodenbach Grand Cru
OUD BRUIN **6.5%** ABV
A sour beer that has been aged in
barrels: very severe and dry; one for
the connoisseur.

Rogue

2320 OSU Drive, Newport,
Oregon 97365, **USA**
www.rogueales.com

Rogue Ales has earned an
international reputation for
brewing envelope-pushing beers
by creating a well-structured malt
foundation on which to layer
massive hop additions. This
approach fostered the growth of
the "Rogue Nation"—loyal fans
who eagerly await the release of
limited-edition beers.

BREWING SECRET Rogue beers are
top-fermented using their own PacMan
yeast which is well suited for bottle-
conditioning.

Shakespeare Stout

STOUT **6**% ABV
Dark, roasted chocolate and coffee
mingle with dark fruits and husky malt.
Substantial, balanced hops and an oily/
creamy smooth finish.

Dead Guy Ale

HELLER BOCK **6.6**% ABV
Complex, clean malt aromas, rich and
fruity, becoming toastier on the palate.
Bright bitter hops. Dry and spicy.

Rooster's

Knaresborough, North Yorkshire,
HG5 8LJ **ENGLAND**
www.roosters.co.uk

The rules are simple:
unconditional care taken in the
selection and preparation of raw
materials is repaid in flavor. Beer
is not an alcoholic commodity to
master brewer Sean Franklin,
but a serious sensory product,
and inventive infusions of
lychees, roses, coffee, grapefruit,
and chocolate are teased from
hop varieties.

Rooster's Yankee
BITTER 4.3% ABV
Aromatic, softly bitter, with aromas of
tropical fruit and Muscat grapes lingering
alongside tangy malt.

Outlaw Wild Mule
BITTER 3.7% ABV
New Zealand hops create a Sauvignon
Blanc wine character in a remarkable and
imposing beer.

Rothaus

Badische Staatsbrauerei Rothaus
AG, Rothaus 1, 79865 Grafenhausen-
Rothaus, **GERMANY**
www.rothaus.de

The Rothaus brewery was
founded in 1791 by the
Benedictine monastery St.
Blasien. Today it is owned by the
State of Baden-Württemberg and
is one of the most profitable
regional breweries in Germany.
Although the brewery does not
advertise, the Tannenzäpfle has
become a cult brand in bars
throughout Germany.

Rothaus Tannenzäpfle

PILSNER 5.1% ABV
Tannenzäpfle ("little fir cones")
is a crisp, elegant, well-rounded pilsner
with a slight final bitterness.

Rothaus Hefeweizen

WHEAT BEER 5.4% ABV
Refreshing top-fermented beer,
with a mild fruity finish.

Rouget de Lisle

Rue des Vernes,
39140 Bletterans, **FRANCE**
www.larougetdelisle.com

Opened in 2002, and named after
the locally born composer of *The
Marseillaise*, this brewery
develops up to 15 new beers each
year, some of them using local
ingredients instead of hops for
their bitter notes.

BREWING SECRET Among the
ingredients used to replace hops are
wormwood, dandelion, blackcurrant,
and gentian.

Fourche Du Diable
LAGER **5.4%** ABV
Amber in color; aromas of spring flowers
and an unusual bitter note contributed by
gentian roots.

Abisinthe
LAGER **6%** ABV
Golden and very refreshing, with aromas
of mint, balm, and the special bitterness
of wormwood.

Rulles

Artisanale de Rulles, 36,
Rue Maurice Grevisse,
B6724 Rulles, **BELGIUM**
www.larulles.be

Seldom does a brand new
brewery (established only in
2000) meet with such immediate
success. Grégory Verhelst's
brews are mesmerizingly
characterful, and the quality of
the labels is equally amazing.

BREWING SECRET Grégory Verhelst
enlisted the help of the Orval brewmaster
to develop his beers.

La Rulles Triple
BELGIAN PALE STRONG ALE 8.4% ABV
No lack of body here; herbal and
dry-bitterness on the palate, yet well
fermented and strong.

La Rulles Estivale
SEASONAL ALE 5.2% ABV
A refreshing, citrussy, blossom-laden
summer ale—one of the best of its kind.

Russian River

1812 Ferdinand Court
Santa Rosa, CA 95404, **USA**
www.russianriverbrewing.com

Owner-brewmaster Vinnie
Cilurzo was the first to brew an
Imperial India Pale Ale
commercially, when he was at
Blind Pig Brewing. That beer is
now called Pliny the Elder and
has become the benchmark for
the style. Cilurzo and his wife,
Natalie, have built a production
brewery separate from their
popular downtown brewpub,
giving more space for a wider
range of barrels and ageing.

Beatification
SOUR ALE 6% ABV
A spontaneously fermented blended beer.
Complex, tart mix of fruit and wood. Just
right acidity at the finish.

Pliny The Elder
IMPERIAL INDIA PALE ALE 8% ABV
Hoppy aroma, hoppy flavor, and a
hoppy bitterness—all supported by
a firm malt base.

Saint Arnold

2522 Fairway Park Drive
Houston, TX 77092, **USA**
www.saintarnold.com

The oldest surviving and largest craft brewery in Texas was founded in 1994. Saint Arnold grew out of its "micro" status in 2007, although it continues to sell its beer only within the state borders. Austrian-born St. Arnold is one of the patron saints of beer; the brewery's fermenters are named after other saints.

Amber

AMBER ALE 5.5% ABV

Caramel and fermentation fruit, with bright, spicy hops providing balance. Excellent on cask.

Elissa IPA

INDIA PALE ALE 6.6% ABV

Delightfully hoppy throughout, brimming with grapefruit character. Big and juicy, with rich malt to match the decided bitterness.

Saint Germain

26 route d'Arras,
62160 Aix-Noulette, **FRANCE**
www.page24.fr

Two young but experienced
brewers opened this brewery in
2003, with top-fermentation
beers in the *bière de garde* style.
One takes its name from Saint
Hildegard, a German abbess of
the 11th century, who is often
(though incorrectly) credited
with the introduction of hops
into the beermaking process.

Reserve Hildegarde Ambrée
ALE **6.9%** ABV

Golden, with a rich nose of cereals,
spices, and honey. Very smooth with
a good bitterness and a long finish.

Page 24 Rhubarbe
ALE **5.9%** ABV

Gold in color, with floral aromas.
Very refreshing, with a special acidity
contributed by rhubarb.

Sainte-Hélène

21, Rue de la Colinne, B6760 Ethe-Belmont, **BELGIUM**
www.sainte-helene.be

After a hectic start, this brewery really got going in 2005, when new brewing equipment was installed. The very southwest corner of Belgium seems to be particularly suited to brewing, as new breweries keep popping up there. Ste-Hélène is enthusiastic about promoting its beers, and is a regular at Belgium's many beer festivals.

La Sainte Hélène Ambrée

BELGIAN AMBER STRONG ALE 8.5% ABV
Close in character to the triple, but with more caramel and tobacco notes; well-balanced.

La Djean Triple

BELGIAN AMBER STRONG ALE 9% ABV
A beer with many flavors and impressions, from phenolic to fruity and dry to creamy.

Samuel Adams

30 Germania Street, Boston,
MA 02130 **USA**
www.samueladams.com

The name Samuel Adams has been
synonymous with craft beer since
Boston Beer Company was one
of just a few specialty beer sellers
in the country. The company
launched the brand in 1984, when
it contracted production to
mainstream producers with excess
capacity. Boston Beer has since
purchased some of those
breweries and produces much of
its own beer. The company holds
an employees' homebrew contest
each year, with the winner's beer
being sold commercially.

Boston Lager

VIENNA LAGER **4.9%** ABV
Complex flowery/piney nose. Full-bodied,
with caramel in the middle, and a
satisfyingly dry finish.

Utopias

STRONG ALE **27%** ABV
The strongest beer in the world, aged in
brandy and port barrels. Serve and sip
like a rare cognac.

Samuel Smith

High Street, Tadcaster, North Yorkshire, LS24 9SB **ENGLAND**
www.tadcaster.uk.com

Tadcaster has three breweries, with "Sam's" by far the smallest—although it can claim to be Yorkshire's oldest. A plentiful supply of water is drawn through limestone from its own wells.

BREWING SECRET Fermentation takes place in traditional slate "Yorkshire squares," which lends distinctive characteristics to flavor and body.

Nut Brown Ale
BROWN ALE 5% ABV

A hazel-colored specialty, with a flavor profile of beech nuts, almonds, and walnuts.

Old Brewery Bitter
BEST BITTER 4% ABV

A typical Northern malty bitter, with a dash of hop and some fruit on the palate.

Schlenkerla

Dominikaner Str. 6,
96049 Bamberg, **GERMANY**
www.schlenkerla.de

This legendary brewery was
known by 1405. Today it is still
a relatively small company, run
by a family in its sixth generation.
The so-called "smoked beer" is
a specialty of Bamberg.

BREWING SECRET The distinctive,
smoky aroma of Schlenkerla's beers
comes from beechwood smoke that
pervades the malt as it dries above
the oven.

Aecht Schlenkerla Rauchbier
MÄRZEN 5.1% ABV
A very dark, dry beer. It has smoky and
roasted malt aromas and a finish of light
hops. A pure pleasure.

Rauchbier Urbock
BOCK 6.5% ABV
A traditional dark bock with
Schlenkerla's trademark smoky and
roasty aromas; dry, malty taste and
a good sweetness in the finish.

BAMBERG, GERMANY

Can there be a better place in the world to drink beer? This beautiful, baroque island city, on the banks of the Regnitz River and the Main-Donau Canal, is in the Upper Franconia region of Bavaria. It is built on medieval foundations and is home to 70,000 people and 11 breweries. The city is a base for many US army personnel and their families—and they have helped, no doubt, to take the fame of this beer paradise around the world.

1 KLOSTERBRAU

Beer has been brewed at Klosterbrau since 1533. Down a cobbled street, time seems to slip away in this fairytale of a brewery tap. The range includes a schwarzbier, braunbier, weizen, pils, and a bock. *Oberre Muhlbruck 3, Bamberg (www.klosterbraueu.de)*

2 OLD TOWN HALL

The river is never far away in Bamberg. The stroll to Brauerei Spezial's passes the spectacular medieval stone-and-timbered Old Town Hall, which seems precariously balanced on the footings of an ancient bridge. Take a moment to admire it before heading on to the Brauerei Spezial's.

3 THE BRAUEREI SPEZIAL'S

The Brauerei Spezial's is very much a locals' bar, decorated with laughter and conversations. Its Specizil Rauchbier has subtle, soft toffee flavors and even a hint of burnt straw. Spezial uses smoked malt in at least four of its other beers. By the bar is a serving hatch, where locals come to fill containers with beer for drinking at home. *Obere Königstrasse 10, Bamberg (www.brauerei-spezial.de)*

4 BRAUEREI FÄSSLA

Directly opposite Brauerei Spezial's is Brauerei Fässla. Brewing started here in 1649. The brewery tap has a comfortable, wood-paneled, country-style room, and above it is a small hotel. The brewery's logo—a dwarf rolling a barrel of beer—decorates the glasses and dark furniture. Fässla's easy-drinking Lagerbier melds malty flavors with a fresh, soft bitterness. *Obere Königsstrasse 19–21, Bamberg (www.faessla.de)*

5 SCHLENKERLA

Vibrant and friendly, Schlenkerla is Bamberg's best-known bar and restaurant. The warmth of its world-famous rauchbier, with its smoked whiskey and cheese overtones, is as warm as the welcome. Tables are often shared, and the atmosphere is highly convivial. Beer is the social lubricant and the perfect accompaniment to robust Bavarian dishes such as onions stuffed with beery meatballs. *Dominikanerstrasse 6, Bamberg (www.smokebeer.com)*

6 AMBRÄUSIANUM

Opposite Schlenkerla is the Ambräusianum. Here, the brewing vessels can be seen, which makes it seem more like a modern brewpub than one of Bamberg's traditional establishments, and it is a relative newcomer, being open only since 2004. Weekend breakfasts comprise a glass of wheat beer with three locally made Bavarian veal sausages and a pretzel. *Dominikanerstrasse 10, Bamberg (www.ambraeusianum.de)*

7 WEINSTUBE PIZZINI

The exterior of the Weinstube Pizzini is somewhat unprepossessing, and do not be deterred by its name—it is neither a wine bar nor a pizza restaurant. Inside this small, brown decorated and time-worn bar, there is a warm-hearted welcome and the opportunity to try Fässla and Spezial beers, as well as a dunkel from Andechser. *Ober Sandstrasse 17, Bamberg*

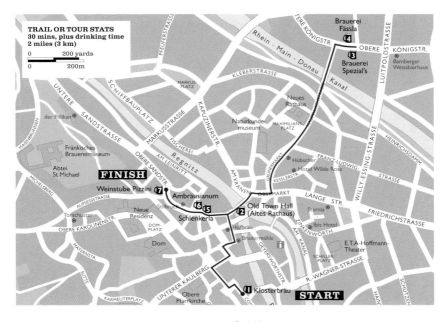

TRAIL OR TOUR STATS
30 mins, plus drinking time
2 miles (3 km)

0   200 yards
0   200m

Schneider

Private Weissbierbrauerei Schneider,
Emil-Ott-Str. 1-5,
93309 Kelheim, **GERMANY**
www.schneider-weisse.de

The Schneider brewery has been
a family-owned company since it
was founded. From its original
location in Munich, Schneider
moved to Kelheim after World
War II. The former brewery in
central Munich has since become
a world-famous restaurant.

Schneider Weisse Original

WHEAT BEER 5.4% ABV
People call it "liquid amber," and they are
right: the amber-mahogany color is
beautiful. Fresh, full-bodied, and with
a light, bitter finish.

Aventinus

STRONG WHEAT BEER 8.2% ABV
Almost black, legendary beer, with
chocolate and dried-fruit aromas;
full-bodied, very thick, and fresh.

Schwechater

Mautner Markhof-Strasse 11,
A-2320 Schwechat, **AUSTRIA**
www.schwechater.at

A large brewery that claims to
have brewed the first lager beer
in 1840, though, to be precise, it
was the Vienna lager that was
invented here by Anton Dreher.
Production of that beer was
discontinued in the early 20th
century. Nowadays the brewery
is part of Heineken and produces
golden lagers.

Schwechater Zwickl
UNFILTERED PILSNER 5.5% ABV
Herbal hop aromas and a hint of lemon
zest. A lot of wheat in the mash bill. Dry
and hoppy finish.

Schwechater Bier
PALE LAGER 5% ABV
Golden color, malty aromas. Full-bodied
with hops being noticeable from the start
to the finish.

Sharp's

Wadebridge, Cornwall,
PL27 6NU **ENGLAND**
www.sharpsbrewery.co.uk

Facing the Atlantic from the Cornish coast undoubtedly has an influence, not only on how the beer is made, but also on people's objectives and horizons. Sharp's commendable approach to sustainable energy and water recycling is echoed by an energetic attitude, which is inspiring for the future of cask ale production.

Doom Bar
BITTER 4% ABV
Spicy resinous hop aromas and sweet, delicate malts blend with dried fruit and assertive bitterness.

Atlantic IPA
INDIA PALE ALE 4.8% ABV
Four hop varieties are added at different stages to create cotton candy aromas and delicate flavors.

Shepherd Neame

Faversham, Kent,
ME13 7AX **ENGLAND**
www.shepherdneame.co.uk

It didn't take 12th-century
monks long to discover that
Faversham's pure spring water
could be combined with locally
grown malting barley to produce
particularly fine ale. When the
town's mayor founded a brewery
in 1698 he launched the country's
longest-surviving brewery,
which was by 1864 called
Shepherd Neame still run
by the Neame family.

BREWING SECRET The brewery still
makes use of mash tuns made from
Russian teak, installed in 1914.

Bishop's Finger
STRONG BITTER 5% ABV
Generously fruity, with banana and pear
prominent, a biscuit-rich maltiness, and
dried fruit flavors.

Spitfire
PREMIUM BITTER 4.5% ABV
A underlying deep maltiness is combined
with a subtle hint of toffee and boldly
fruity citrus hops.

Shiga Kogen

1163 Hirao, Yamanouchi-machi,
Shimo Takai-gun Nagano 381-0401,
JAPAN
www.tamamura-honten.co.jp

In September 2004, saké brewer
Tamamura Honten broke a little
of their 200-year tradition and
began brewing beer. Within three
years Shiga Kogen had become
one of the most respected
Japanese craft beer brands. Clear
product identity and superior
label designs have contributed
to the beer's popularity.

House DPA / Draft Pale Ale

PALE ALE 8% ABV

American in style, with a brilliant
orange-gold hue, complex floral hop
aroma, and lingering sweetness.

Miyama Blonde

SAISON-LIKE BEER 7% ABV

Made using the Miyama Nishiki strain
of saké rice, along with European hops
and barley. Rich and interesting, but with
a brisk finish.

Shiner

603 Brewery Street
Shiner, TX 77984, **USA**
www.shiner.com

Founded in 1909, the Spoetzl
Brewery has ridden the success
of Shiner Bock into national
prominence. In 2004 it began
counting down toward its 100th
birthday by releasing a special
new beer every year, each one
reflecting a German heritage that
dates back to the original Shiner
Brewing Association.

Shiner Hefeweizen

HEFEWEIZEN 5.3% ABV
Cloudy, brewed in the Bavarian style
with a bit of honey added. More wheat
character than yeast, with a hint of citrus.

Shiner Bock

US DARK LAGER 4.4% ABV
A dark lager, rather than a true German
bock. Hints of caramel sweetness.
Deliberately low on hops.

Shongweni / Robson's

B1 Shongweni Valley, Shongweni,
near Durban, KwaZulu-Natal,
SOUTH AFRICA
www.shongwenibrewery.com

Shongweni mainly produces
bottle-conditioned beers, using
the infusion mash technique and
fermentation in open-top vessels.
All its beers are unfiltered and
unpasteurized. The family-owned
brewery stands out in a local
market dominated by mass-
produced lagers. It exports to
the UK and elsewhere.

Robson's Durban Pale Ale
INDIA PALE ALE 5.7% ABV
Brewed with Pale malt, and Cascade and
Challenger hops. Crisp, fruity, and
well-balanced.

Robson's East Coast Ale
GOLDEN ALE 4% ABV
A smooth and refreshing golden
ale, made with a single malt variety along
with Brewers Gold and Challenger hops.

Siebensternbräu

Siebensterngasse 19,
A-1070 Vienna, **AUSTRIA**
www.7stern.at

Siebensternbräu was the first
brewpub in Austria to brew
specialty beers—IPA, chili,
and fruit flavored. Owner Sigi
Flitter also helped reintroduce
many of Austria's indigenous but
forgotten beer styles.

BREWING SECRET The range varies
with each season, but expect a wheat beer
in summer and a smoked in winter.

Rauchbock
SMOKED BOCK 7.9% ABV
Intense smoky nose; full, almost sweet
body, with hints of chocolate and
liquorice, and a smoky finish.

Prager Dunkles
DARK LAGER 4.5% ABV
While most dark beers in Austria are
terribly sweet, this one is dry. Intense
toasty notes, very little hop aroma.
Roasty finish.

Sierra Nevada

1075 East 20th Street, Chico,
CA 95928, **USA**
www.sierranevada.com

Sierra Nevada Brewing has been introducing beer drinkers to citrusy, piney Northwest hops since 1981 and the brewery continues to act as a matchmaker between beer drinkers and hops. Sierra Nevada is also an industry leader in good environmental practice. It has commissioned the first phase of one of the country's largest private solar installations, which will bring it close to its goal of generating 100 percent of its energy needs.

Pale Ale

PALE ALE **5.6**% ABV

Piney, grapefruity Cascade hops play against malt fruitiness on both the nose and the palate.

Bigfoot

BARLEY WINE **9.6**% ABV

Earthy and chewy, with prominent citric hops and whiskeylike rich malts. Boldly bitter when young.

Silly / Mynsbrug Hen

2, Ville Basse, B7830 Silly, **BELGIUM**
www.silly-beer.com

Established in the 19th century, this family brewery walks a fine line between maintaining traditions and employing technical developments geared toward satisfying changing market niches. A *saison* is still produced—bottled and, better yet, on draft—and they have recently launched a beer flavored with rum and named after a regional rock band.

Silly Saison

SAISON 5.2% ABV
Fruity, madeiralike, thin-bodied. Even when young, this is more like an oud bruin than a real *saison*.

Scotch Silly

SCOTCH ALE 8% ABV
Scotch ales are a Walloon tradition. This very malty dark beer is full-bodied and rich.

Simonds Farsons Cisk

The Brewery, Notabile Road,
Mriehel, BKR 01, **MALTA**
www.farsons.com

Wherever the British army went,
beer was soon to follow, and this
brewery was built in lavish Art
Deco style at the end of World
War II in 1946. The site is being
redeveloped, with the old
brewing vessels at the heart of a
visitor center.

BREWING SECRET It brews the potent
XS (9% ABV) for the export market.

Farsons Lacto

MILK STOUT 3.8% ABV

Soft on the tongue, this black beer is a
classic milk stout, with lactose added
after fermentation.

Hopleaf Extra

ALE 5% ABV

English malt, along with Challenger and
Target hops, produce a complex beer with
a refreshing bitter finish.

Sinebrychoff

Oy Sinebrychoff Ab,
Sinebrychoffinaukio 1 PL 87,
FL-04201 Kerava, **FINLAND**
www.koff.fi

Sinebrychoff is part of the
Carlsberg Group, and its
abbreviated name and main
brand range, Koff, is one of the
most popular in Finland. It is the
oldest Nordic brewery, founded
by Russian Nikolai Sinebrychoff
in 1819.

BREWING SECRET Karhupanimo, their
new microbrewery, is producing a range
of hand-crafted lagers.

Sinebrychoff Porter
IMPERIAL STOUT **7.2%** ABV
Robust and brimming with coffee flavors,
this beer has a long, warming finish.

Karhu III
LAGER **4.6%** ABV
Described by the brewer as "untamed."
Full-bodied, with stronger flavors of hops
and malt than are usual for a lager.

Ska

545 Turner Drive
Durango, CO 81301, **USA**
www.skabrewing.com

Bill Graham and Dave Thibodeau
named their brewery for the
Jamaican music they played
while homebrewing in college,
reflecting their motto "it takes
characters to brew beer with
character." When they founded
Ska in 1995, they had day jobs
and brewed at night. Now they
can't keep up with the demand
for their beers and are building
a new brewery.

Ten Pin Porter

PORTER 5.4% ABV

Chocolate and caramel throughout, with
roasted coffee stronger in the flavor.
Eases into bitterness.

True Blonde

GOLDEN ALE 4.2% ABV

Brewed with honey made just north of
town. Light biscuity malt, hints of honey,
and a touch of citric hops.

Sleeman

551 Clair Road West, Guelph,
Ontario, N1L 1E9, **CANADA**
www.sleeman.com

The Sleeman family started
brewing in Canada in 1834, the
year John Sleeman, an ambitious
young brewer from England,
arrived in Ontario. In 1851
he started the first Guelph-based
Sleeman Brewery, making small,
100-barrel batches with local well
water, prized for its purity and
hardness. The company is now
owned by Sapporo.

Honey Brown Lager

LAGER 5% ABV

A refreshingly smooth, full-bodied lager,
with a subtle touch of honey which
creates a slightly sweet finish.

Sleeman Cream Ale

ALE 5% ABV

Designed to combine the refreshing
quality of German lager with the
distinctive taste of English Ale.

Smuttynose

225 Heritage Avenue
Portsmouth, NH 03801, **USA**
www.smuttynose.com

Although Smuttynose Brewing
has earned a reputation for its
carefully balanced offerings, the
brewery was also one of the first
to embrace "extreme beers,"
launching a Big Beer Series in
1998. Succeeding on all fronts, it
found itself out of room by 2007,
and plans to relocate its brewing,
still close to Portsmouth.

Shoals Pale Ale
PALE ALE 5% ABV
First made at the Portsmouth pub.
Pleasant fruity/biscuit palate gives
way to a crisp American hop finish.

Robust Porter
PORTER 5.7% ABV
Rich dark fruits and chocolate, well
blended throughout. Rich, roasty flavors
leave a strong impression for a medium-
strength beer.

Snake River

265 S. Millward Street
Jackson, WY 83001, **USA**
www.snakeriverbrewing.com

Located in central Jackson, with
a view of Snow King Mountain
and standing but a few miles
from the Jackson Hole ski resort,
Snake River brewpub occupies an
old cinder-block warehouse. It
has twice won Small Brewery of
the Year at the Great American
Beer Festival.

Zonker Stout
STOUT 5.8% ABV
Roasted barley sets a bold tone, with
chocolate (almost sweet) underneath.
Pleasingly dry finish.

Lager
VIENNA LAGER 6% ABV
Golden, with a thick white head.
Malt-accented, clean toasted and
caramel flavors, drying hop finish.

Southampton

40 Bowden Square
Southampton, NY 11968, **USA**
www.publick.com

Southampton Publick House's busy brewmaster, Phil Markowski, routinely travels to three breweries in New York State and Pennsylvania to make Southampton-branded beer. As well as the eclectic range he's created for the brewery-restaurant on Long Island, he also brews specials, packaged in 750ml corked bottles, and oversees the production of Double White and Secret Ale. Since early 2008, the Southampton range of beers has been marketed by Pabst.

Saison

SAISON **6.5%** ABV
An endorsement for "Farmhouse Ales"—fruity, peppery, slightly tart, earthy, and refreshing.

Secret Ale

ALTBIER **5.1%** ABV
Slightly sweet caramel aromas, with firm bitterness matching rich malt on the palate, lasting beyond the finish.

Starobrno

Hlinky 160/12, 661 47 Brno,
CZECH REPUBLIC
www.starobrno.cz

Brewing around Brno began in monasteries and convents, notably those of the Augustinian Brothers and Cistercian Sisters. The highest production and technical standards—features of its Mandell and Huzak family ownership since 1872—have earned Starobrno a coveted "Czech Made" quality certificate. It is now owned by Dutch firm Heineken.

Starobrno Premium Lager
PREMIUM LAGER **4**% ABV
A nose of hay, melon, and malt, then heightening traces of caramel on the palate.

Starobrno Rezák
DARK BEER **4**% ABV
A deep amber Vienna-style lager unveiling slight bitter hop and joyous caramel mouthfuls.

Staropramen

Nádražni 84, 150 54 Prague 5,
CZECH REPUBLIC
www.staropramen.com

Far-sighted developers situated the Smíchov Brewery in Prague's future industrial area, where demand for beer was assured. From the start, Staropramen—Prague's biggest brewer—was perceived as a Czech beer for Czech people, which gave it an advantage among nationalist-leaning consumers. Today it is owned by global giant InBev.

Staropramen Dark Beer
DARK BEER 4.5% ABV
Its light body loops around malty caramel, liquorice, and aniseed notes to a floral finale.

Staropramen Premium Lager
PREMIUM LAGER 5% ABV
A rich floral bite unveils a full-bodied satisfier with a riz ("just right") finish.

St. Austell

St. Austell, Cornwall,
PL25 4BY **ENGLAND**
www.staustellbrewery.co.uk

The enterprising spirit that
drove Walter Hicks to mortgage
his farm for £1,500 in 1851 and
set up a brewery remains at the
core of today's business. Many
of his descendants are still
involved in the company—in
its estate of 168 pubs and in
the brewery, which produces
in excess of 40,000 barrels
(6.5 million liters) annually.

Tribute
BITTER **4.2**% ABV
Specially grown Cornish Gold barley
delivers a rich biscuit aroma, tempered by
intense fruit flavors.

St. Austell IPA
INDIA PALE ALE **3.4**% ABV
Full of flavor and packed with fresh
hoppiness; the rounded palate arrives
with veils of caramel.

St Christoffel

Metaalweg 10, 6045 JB Roermond,
NETHERLANDS
www.christoffelbier.nl

Operating since 1986, St
Christoffel is one of the oldest
Dutch micros, founded (but no
longer run) by Leo Brand, a
member of the Brand brewing
dynasty. It produces the very
best lagers brewed in
the Netherlands.

BREWING SECRET The Robertus beer is
a rare example of a Münchner dark lager
that's true to the Bavarian style.

Christoffel Blond
PILS **6**% ABV
Spicy hop flavors burst from the glass
—basil, mint, ginger, grapefruit, and
cloves are all there.

Christoffel Robertus
MÜNCHNER **6**% ABV
The nutty flavor of Munich malt runs
right through this beer, flanked by
biscuit, toast, and toffee.

Stiegl

Kendlerstrasse 1,
A-5017 Salzburg, **AUSTRIA**
www.stiegl.at

Austria's largest independent
brewery produces Austria's
single most successful beer,
Goldbräu. The brewery itself
dates back to 1492 and, over
time, has built up a splendid
collection of beer-related exhibits
for the "Brauwelt"—the largest
museum on the continent
entirely devoted to brewing.

Goldbräu
AUSTRIAN MÄRZEN-TYPE
LAGER 4.9% ABV
Relatively low bitterness and a hint
of malty sweetness in the aroma and
on the palate.

Paracelsus Zwickl
ORGANIC LAGER 5% ABV
Unfiltered, so hazy orange in hue; aromas
of malt and yeast; medium body and very
low bitterness.

Brauhaus Sternen

Hohenzornstrasse 2, CH-8500
Frauenfeld, **SWITZERLAND**
www.brauhaussternen.ch

This is an intriguing brewpub,
set up on the site of the
Aktienbrauerei Frauenfeld,
where Martin Wartmann created
Ittinger (now brewed at Calanda).
The present brewery was built in
2003 with financial help from
many prominent European
brewers eager to see Martin brew
interesting beers, some in limited
editions ("Nur für Freunde"—
"for friends only").

Wartmann's Nur Für Freunde No1
BELGIAN DUBBEL 9.6% ABV
Chocolaty, slightly sweet aroma. Full-
bodied and fruity (ripe plums); very mild
bitterness in the finish.

Honey Brown Ale
BROWN ALE 6% ABV
Sweet and fruity. Quite refreshing for its
strength. Very low bitterness and a hint
of honey in the finish.

Stiftsbrauerei Schlägl

Schlägl 1, A-4160 Schlägl, **AUSTRIA**
www.stift-schlaegl.at

The small village of Schlägl, close to the Czech and Bavarian borders, is home to the only Austrian brewery wholly owned by a monastery—in this case the Premonstratensian order. In recent years the product range has grown considerably and now includes several ales.

Stifter Bier
RED ALE 5.7% ABV
Malty sweetness with a refreshing fruit (peach and melon) undertone. Just a faint hint of hops.

Doppelbock
DOPPELBOCK 8.3% ABV
A big, malty nose. Fruity (pears and apples) and sweet from the start, but very well-balanced finish.

Stone

1999 Citracado Parkway
Escondido, CA 92029, **USA**
www.stonebrew.com

Although some find the "you are
not worthy" campaign, used to
promote Arrogant Bastard Ale,
off putting, CEO Greg Koch's
argument in favor of particularly
full-flavored beers is the opposite
of elitist. He doesn't think beer
appreciation takes special skill:
"If you want to turn people on to
great beer, use great beer to do
it," he says. That philosophy has
resulted in 30 percent annual
growth year after year, and a
larger brewery, built in 2006.

IPA

INDIA PALE ALE 6.9% ABV

Fruity hop aromas meet firm malt
character at the start, developing
complexity, finishing bitter but bright.

Imperial Russian Stout

IMPERIAL STOUT 9.4% ABV

Intense, full of chocolate, roasted coffee,
and dark fruits. All balanced by a
brooding bitterness.

Sul Brasileira

BR 392, Km 05, Santa Maria—
RS, 97000, **BRAZIL**

Local folklore says that Sul
Brasileira's Xingu beer is the
daughter of a beer brewed in
ancient times by pioneering
Amazonian brewsters. The name
Xinghu (pronounced "shin-goo")
is a tributary of the Amazon
River, which is home to the few
surviving cultures and species
of native Amazonian life.

Xingu Black Beer
SCHWARZBIER 4.7% ABV
Dark in color, but light and sweet
to taste. Still in the glass, its head
soon disappears.

Švyturys-Utenos

Kuliu Vartu g. 7, Klaipeda,
LITHUANIA
www.svyturys.lt/en

Brewing began here in 1784,
making this the oldest brewery in
Lithuania. The company has a
reputation for the quality of its
beers and has won several
international brewing awards. It
is open to the public for tours
twice a week for groups of five to
25 (via the tourist office at www.
klaipedainfo.lt).

BREWING SECRET All the employees
give their feedback on each new brew.

Švyturys Ekstra
DORTMUND LAGER 5.2% ABV
Clear and golden, it has a firm white
head, an intense aroma of hops, and a
slight bitterness.

Švyturio
LAGER 5% ABV
Translucent gold in color, it has a good
balance of rich malt and bitter hops. In
Lithuania it's known simply as "red," due
to its label color.

Teerenpeli

Hämeenkatu 19, Lahti, **FINLAND**
www.teerenpeli.com

Teerenpeli operates breweries,
bars, and restaurants in
Helsinki, Lahti, and Tampere.
Its first brewery was founded
in 1995. A new brewery and
whiskey distillery opened in
2002, set within the Restaurant
Taivaanranta in Lahti.
Teerenpeli's beers have
won medals at the Helsinki
Beer Festival.

Laiskajaakko
DARK LAGER 4.5% ABV
Full-bodied, malty dark lager, brewed
with Crystal 50 and Black malt, and
Hallertau hops.

Onnenpekka
PALE LAGER 4.7% ABV
Golden and refreshing. Made with Pilsner
barley malt from the Lahti region, and
pure water from the Salpausselkä area.

Terrapin

255 Newton Bridge Road
Athens, GA 30607, **USA**
www.terrapinbeer.com

Spike Buckowski and John
Cochran began shipping beer
from their own brewhouse early
in 2008, almost six years after
the Terrapin Beer Company
started selling contract-brewed
Rye Pale Ale. That beer was an
immediate hit, as was the
Monster Beer Tour, a series of
strong beers released after
Georgia raised its 6 percent
ABV cap on beer.

Rye Pale Ale

PALE ALE 5.3% ABV
Rye blends with bright grapefruit, adds
texture to fruit fermentation, and
complements late bitterness.

Wake-n-Bake Coffee Oatmeal Imperial Stout

IMPERIAL STOUT 8.1% ABV
It's all in the name, along with
chocolate-covered dark fruits.

Theakston

Masham, North Yorkshire,
HG4 4YD **ENGLAND**
www.theakstons.co.uk

Ownership battles may have swept in numerous changes during its 180-year history but, fortunately today, tradition survives and thrives. Now returned to the Theakston family following Scottish & Newcastle's management, the company lives up to the name of its most famous beer— Peculier, a 12th-century word meaning "particular."

Old Peculier
STRONG BITTER 5.6% ABV
Rich and deep dark ruby in hue, with a mellow fruit aroma and a malty, full-bodied flavor.

Black Bull Bitter
BITTER 3.9% ABV
Bright amber colored, with a crisp, dry palate weaving through citrus fruit flavors.

Thiriez

22 rue de Wormhout,
59470 Esquelbecq, **FRANCE**
http://brasseriethiriez.ifrance.com

From working as a manager in
a food distribution company,
Daniel Thiriez changed his life
to become an artisan brewer.
He established his brewery
on an old farm in Flanders in
1996, and uses traditional
brewing methods.

BREWING SECRET Thiriez's unfiltered
beers have a second fermentation in
the bottle, on their lees.

Étoile Du Nord
BLOND ALE 5.5% ABV
The moment the bottle is opened, an
extraordinary smell of fresh hops
comes to the nose. The beer's refreshing
bitterness is in perfect harmony
with its fine malt aromas.

Thornbridge

Bakewell, Derbyshire,
DE45 1NZ **ENGLAND**
www.thornbridgebrewery.co.uk

Resounding success has followed
from the brewery's philosophy of
being "never ordinary." While
brewing heritage is of prime
importance, innovation,
enthusiasm, experience, and a
commitment to creating new
and exciting recipes have driven
the business since it was
established in 2005 in the
grounds of Thornbridge Hall
country manor house.

Jaipur

INDIA PALE ALE **5.9**% ABV
Tantalizingly complex; emphasis on
citrus hoppiness; its powerful length
develops a bitter finish.

Lord Marples

BITTER **4**% ABV
Easy-drinking bitter, with hints of honey
and caramel, and a long, bitter afterglow.

Three Boys Brewery

Unit 10, Garlands Rd, Woolston,
Christchurch, **NEW ZEALAND**
www.threeboysbrewery.co.nz

Microbiologist Ralph Bungard
employs a broad range of
yeasts to produce tasty Kiwi
interpretations of classic beer
styles. The senior "Boy"—the
others are his sons Marek
and Quinn.

BREWING SECRET The brewery's
limited release seasonal brews include
an excellent Oyster Stout in winter and
a fragrant Golden Ale in summer.

Three Boys Wheat
WITBIER 5% ABV
Plenty of zesty lemon and coriander
notes, with a hint of ginger.
A spritzy and quenching brew.

Three Boys Porter
ROBUST PORTER 5.2% ABV
Rich mocha notes dominate a silky
palate, while heavily roasted grain
and hops compete in the dry finish.

Three Floyds

9750 Indiana Parkway
Munster, IN 46321, **USA**
www.threefloyds.com

Beginning with its flagship
Alpha King in 1996, Three
Floyds Brewing had lived by
the philosophy of brewmaster
Nick Floyd: "I love the smell of
hops in the morning. It smells
like victory."

BREWING SECRET The annual release
of Dark Lord Russian Imperial Stout sells
out in one day, with customers driving
hundreds of miles to buy it.

Alpha King
PALE ALE 6% ABV
Opens with a rush of citrus fruits. Firm
malt backbone, matched by hop oils.
Prolonged bitterness.

Gumballhead
US WHEAT BEER 4.8% ABV
Citrus and orchard fruits on the
nose, followed by wheat tartness and
hops throughout.

Timmermans

Kerkstraat 11, B1701 Itterbeek,
BELGIUM
www.anthonymartin.be/Public/

Once a traditional lambic
brewery, Timmermans was
among the first to habitually
mix top-fermented beer into its
blends. The brewery has also
been eager to produce all kinds
of syrup-lambic concoctions,
designed to appeal more to
the younger generation.
Timmermans products, including
Tradition, are easily found in
Belgian supermarkets.

Tradition Gueuze

GUEUZE 5% ABV

Once known as "Caveau," this beer is a
mix of tradition and commercialism, and
so are its flavors: more pineapple than
citrus, and herbal rather than the typical
horse blanket notes.

Timothy Taylor

Keighley, West Yorkshire,
BD21 1AW **ENGLAND**
www.timothy-taylor.co.uk

The Taylor family guides the
enterprise, as it has done since
the brewery's inception in 1858.

BREWING SECRET Pure Pennine water
from the brewery's own spring is a
natural companion to the Golden Promise
barley (also used extensively for malt
whiskey); together, they form the
legendary "Taylor's taste."

Landlord

PREMIUM BITTER **4.3**% ABV
Complex hoppy aroma, well-balanced
spice and citrus fruit flavors, tinged
with biscuit malt.

Best Bitter

BEST BITTER **4**% ABV
A full measure of maltiness following
citrus fruit, hoppy aromas define an
honest Yorkshire bitter.

Titanic

**Burslem, Staffordshire,
ST6 1JL ENGLAND**
www.titanicbrewery.co.uk

What began with brewing for
demonstration purposes on
log-fired Victorian equipment
developed into the production of
in excess of 17 million pints a
year. Ecologically friendly
business practices—recycling
and conservation—are a priority.
The name is taken from the
world's most famous passenger
ship, whose captain, John
Edward Smith, was born nearby.

Titanic Stout
STOUT 4.5% ABV
Full roast, preserved fruit aromas; the
malt-influenced palate accentuates more
fruit and liquorice tiers.

Best Bitter
BEST BITTER 3.5% ABV
Straw colored, with a waft of sulfur in the
aroma and persistent hop flavorings.

Topvar

Krusovska cesta 2092,
Topolcany, **SLOVAKIA**
www.topvar.sk

The brewery operates at two sites
in Slovakia: Topolcany and Velký
Šariš. In 2000, the brewery
launched a beer called Brigita,
named after the Slovak finance
minister Brigita Schmögnerovà.
A popular beer, it remained on
sale for some time after her
resignation in 2002. The company
is now owned by SABMiller.

Topvar Svetlé
LAGER 5.2% ABV

A sunburst of yellow tones, with a thin
white head. This beer has an attractive
nose, with plenty of citrus fruit flavors.

Traquair

Innerleithen, Peeblesshire,
EH44 6PW **SCOTLAND**
www.traquair.co.uk

The 18th-century brewing
equipment in a house where
Bonnie Prince Charlie once
sought refuge remained
untouched until their rediscovery
in 1965. Since then, they have
been put to use for brewing in
authentic style.

BREWING SECRET Unusually in this
day and age, Traquair's beers are
fermented in oak over a seven-day period.

Traquair House Ale
BARLEY WINE 7.2% ABV
A dark and oaky winter brew, with ripe
malt, fruit cake, and sweet sherry
mystique.

Jacobite Ale
BARLEY WINE 8% ABV
Herbal notes from the use of coriander
warm the bittersweet chocolate and port
wine flavors.

La Trappe

Eindhovenseweg 3, Berkel-Enschot,
NETHERLANDS
www.latrappe.nl

There are just seven genuine
Trappist breweries in the world;
Koningshoeven (better known as
La Trappe) is the only one outside
Belgium. The monastery had
problems recruiting new monks,
and that was one of the factors
that prompted the sale of the
brewery to Bavaria. Brewing still
takes place within the monastery
grounds under the supervision
of the monks.

La Trappe Witte Trappist
WITBIER 5.5% ABV
Unspiced, but a subtle use of aromatic
hops more than compensates, providing
delicious citrus and pepper flavors.

La Trappe Tripel
STRONG ALE 8% ABV
Sweetness and fruit give way to coriander,
orange, and hop bitterness in this
supremely balanced beer.

Tsingtao

Hong Kong Road, Central,
Qinqdao, 266071 **CHINA**
www.tsingtaobeer.com

The Tsingtao Brewery was
founded in 1903 by German
settlers in Qingdao. Today it is
part owned by American giants
Anheuser Busch, which is
currently undertaking a massive
investment in new breweries on
the China mainland. The
company runs over 40 breweries
and malt plants in 18 provinces
across China.

Tsingtao
LAGER 4.8% ABV

Crisp, slightly malty flavor and nutty
sweet taste. The color is a bright
yellow; aroma grainy, with a hint of
sweetness. A high level of carbonation
makes it very fizzy.

U Medvídků

Na Perštýně 7, 100 01 Prague 1,
CZECH REPUBLIC
www.umedvidku.cz

The restaurant and brewhouse
date back to 1466, though the
brewery has been reinstalled in
recent years—along with
extensions and additions to the
pension, which retains its
original Gothic rafters and
Renaissance painted ceilings.
This is one of the biggest beer
halls in Prague, and it hosted the
city's first cabaret.

Oldgott Barique Ležák
PILSNER 5.2% ABV
Earthy and melon-fruity aromas, yeasty
characteristics developing into a roasted
malt, caramel infusion.

X-Beer
SPECIALTY BEER 12.6% ABV (VARIABLE)
Matured for 28 weeks in oak vessels
for an elaborate, sweet flavor and
indulgent complexity.

Union

Pivovarniška ulica 2,
1000 Ljubljana, **SLOVENIA**
www.pivo-union.si

This brewery was founded in 1864 by the Kozler family, but state-of-the-art technology makes it one of the most modern in Slovenia. A fascinating museum takes visitors through the brewing process. However, you have to be there on the first Tuesday morning of the month to enjoy it.

Union Lager
LAGER 5% ABV
A Slovenian favorite. A sweet, golden beer, it has corn overtones.

ČRNI Baron / Black Baron
STOUT 5.2% ABV
A dark dessert beer, rich with caramel notes and aromas; its finish is warming but could be longer.

United Breweries

Bengaluru, **INDIA**
www.theubgroup.com

It is said the company's logo—
a Pegasus—once carried a cask
of beer between its wings as a gift
to the gods. Its Kingfisher brand
is the flying leader in India's
soaring beer market, and what
once was a company that
supplied beer to the troops of the
British Empire has now acquired
a worldwide reputation.

Kingfisher

LAGER 5% ABV
Brewed under license in many
countries. It has a crisp taste with a
sweetish overtone.

London Pilsner 5.0

LAGER 5% ABV
Thin yellow color, some hop aroma, and a
sweetish after taste, it smells of grass.

Upstream

514 South 11th Street
Omaha, NE 68102, **USA**
www.upstreambrewing.com

Since opening in 1996 as part of an "unlinked chain" started by Wynkoop Brewery, Upstream (a translation of the Native American name for Omaha) has gained independence, opened a second pub, and brewed varieties of beers not previously found in Nebraska.

BREWING SECRET Developments include barrel-ageing, and the use of wild yeast.

Batch 1000 Barley Wine

BARLEY WINE **10.2%** ABV
Caramel and vinous on the nose and palate, blending with lively fruity esters. Rich, almost chewy, palate.

Grand Cru

BELGIAN STRONG ALE 9% ABV
Aged for a year in oak wine barrels. Earthy and woody nose, delicate citrus and honey on the palate, ultimately balanced.

Vancouver Island

2330 Government St, Victoria, British Colombia, V8T 5G5, **CANADA**
www.vanislandbrewery.com

The inspiration for this company's formation in 1984 was the absence of locally made beers on Vancouver Island. The brewery believes that brewing should be a perfect blend of art and science, with no short cuts.

BREWING SECRET Though the hops and yeast are imported, only the finest Canadian barley is used.

Hermannator
EISBOCK 9.5% ABV
Brewed and then frozen, it is a symphony of complex chestnut colors and spicy flavors.

Hermann's Dark
BAVARIAN LAGER 5.5% ABV
A toasty malt nose with similar flavors on the palate; takes on a somewhat nutty character.

Victory

420 Acorn Lane
Downingtown, PA 19335, **USA**
www.victorybeer.com

Victory Brewing founders Ron
Barchet and Bill Covaleski—who
met on a school bus in 1973—
traveled much of the beer world,
apprenticed in Germany, and
worked in US micro breweries
before starting their own in
1996. The breadth of their
interests is reflected in the
range of their beers.

BREWING SECRET Victory has long-
term contracts with German hop-growers
to assure the availability of authentic
ingredients for their lagers.

Prima Pils
PILSNER 5.3% ABV
Fresh flowery aromas, cookielike palate,
and a solidly bitter-rough finish. Sturdy
yet delicate.

Golden Monkey
TRIPLE 9.5% ABV
Spicy, with hints of banana followed by
light pepper. Candy-sweet on the palate,
with a dry finish.

Wadworth

Devises, Wiltshire,
SN10 1JW **ENGLAND**
www.wadworth.co.uk

Established by Henry Wadworth,
the brewery began producing
beer in 1875 and was expanded
10 years later into an impressive,
red-brick Victorian tower
brewery. The original open
copper is still operational and
wooden casks are used for local
deliveries. A full-time cooper and
a team of dray horses continue
traditional customs.

Wadworth 6X

BEST BITTER 4.3% ABV
A malt and fruit nose, with restrained
hop characteristics developing an
intensity on the palate.

JEB

STRONG BITTER 4.7% ABV
Aromatic wafts of tropical fruit; a rich
malt mouth with some nutty sweetness
on the palate.

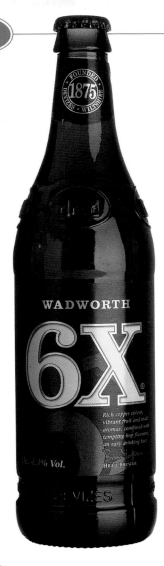

Weitra Bräu

Sparkassaplatz 160,
A-3970 Weitra, **AUSTRIA**
www.bierwerkstatt.at

Weitra claims to hold Austria's oldest brewing privilege, issued in 1321. In medieval times, most of the buildings around the town square exercised their right to brew, now there is only one brewpub and this brewery left.

BREWING SECRET This organic specialty brewery, bought by Zwettler in 2002, still brews using open fermenters.

Hadmar
ORGANIC VIENNA LAGER 5.2% ABV
Sweet and malty on the nose and palate; hints of roastyness, bitterness; variable from batch to batch.

Weitra Hell
LAGER 5% ABV
Straw colored, with estery aroma and very little carbonation. Soft on the palate, with a mild hoppyness.

Wells & Young's

Bedford, Bedfordshire,
MK40 4LU **ENGLAND**
www.charleswells.co.uk
www.youngs.co.uk

A major force in British brewing
was created in 2006 from the
partnership of London brewer
Young's and Bedford-based
Charles Wells, two of the most
prodigiously accomplished
operators in the industry. Wells &
Young's cask and bottled ale
portfolio is one of the broadest in
the brewing sector, particularly
after Courage brands—Best Bitter
and Directors Bitter—were added
in 2007 under an agreement with
Scottish & Newcastle.

Wells Bombardier
PREMIUM BITTER 4.3% ABV
Powerful citrus hop aromas meet
malt and dried fruit in a richly
complex medley.

Young's Bitter
BITTER 3.7% ABV
Well-balanced, with citrus hop notes
and enough malt for a flowery and
bready finish.

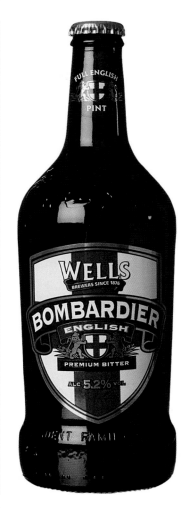

Weltenburg

Klosterbaruerei Weltenburg,
Heitzerstr. 2, 93049 Regensburg,
GERMANY
www.weltenburger.de

The Benedictine abbey of
Weltenburg houses the oldest
abbey brewery in the world,
founded in 1050. The location
is delightful, close to the scenic
Donau-Durchbruch gorge.
The abbey's restaurant is famous.

BREWING SECRET Despite its history,
the beer is made with the most advanced
equipment, but is long-matured.

Asam Bock
BOCK **6.9%** ABV
A dark mahogany doppelbock. Very
pleasant, it tastes slightly sweet with
nice malty aromas in the finish.

Anno 1050
EXPORT **5.5%** ABV
The abbey's anniversary beer has
a distinctive mix of malt aromas
balanced with hops.

Westmalle

Antwerpsesteenweg 496,
B2390 Malle, **BELGIUM**
www.trappistwestmalle.be

Monks started brewing here in
1836, selling beer at the gate 20
years later. Today, the abbey
operates one of the world's most
modern breweries, hidden behind
the old brewhouse. Westmalle has
come to define abbey ales
through their "Dubbel" and
"Tripel" styles. The "Extra" could
be another world classic, if the
monks were to commercialize it.

Westmalle Dubbel
ABBEY ALE 7% ABV
Dark and vinous, with sugar sweetness
coming through; surprisingly hoppy.
A classic.

Westmalle Tripel
ABBEY ALE 9.5% ABV
The dry Champenoise triple that made all
triples blonde. Sweetish and fruity, with a
hoppy finish.

Westvleteren

Donkerstraat 12,
B8640 Vleteren, **BELGIUM**
www.sintsixtus.be

The Abbey of St. Sixtus of
Westvleteren is the reclusive star
of the beer world. It sells its beer
by telephone reservation only—
unwillingly even—as if to
emphasize that the operation is
run by monks who brew in order
to be able to pray, instead of pray
in order to sell. Westvleteren
voluntarily limits production.

BREWING SECRET This is the only
remaining Trappist brewery that still
employs solely in-house monks.

Westvleteren Blond
ABBEY ALE 5.8% ABV
A blonde ale that starts with a big grain
flavor, followed by very serious hops;
best bitterlike.

Westvleteren ABT 12°
ABBEY ALE 10.2% ABV
A truly massive dark Trappist ale:
chewy like no other beer, and with a
perfect balance between the sweet and
bitter notes.

Wickwar

Wickwar, Gloucestershire,
GL12 8NB **ENGLAND**
www.wickwarbrewing.co.uk

A million-pound refurbishment
has hoisted Wickwar from
microbrewery status to regional
heights, increasing its brewing
capacity almost fourfold. Beers
are matured in below-ground
vaults at the former Arnold
Perret & Co. Brewery. The export
market is an increasing area
of interest, with encouraging
European sales.

Station Porter
PORTER **6.1%** ABV
Richly smooth, with roast coffee,
chocolate, and dried fruits combining
with complex spiced flavors.

IKB
BEST BITTER **4.7%** ABV
Bold in its multi-malt flavors, with rich
cherry and plum fruit breaking through.

Widmer

929 North Russell
Portland, OR 97227, **USA**
www.widmer.com

More than two decades old, the
US-centric Hefeweizen (cloudy
but accented by yeast rather than
hops) that the Widmer brothers
basically invented continues to
drive double-digit growth.
Widmer and Redhook have
merged to form a single
company called Craft Breweries
Alliance, but Widmer maintains
its own brewery.

Hefeweizen
US HEFEWEIZEN 4.9% ABV
Citrus, particularly lemon zest, is
matched against clean, bready-yet-tart
wheat. Finale of grapefruit.

Snow Plow
MILK STOUT 5.5% ABV
Coffee on the nose becomes creamier on
the palate, roasted notes blending with
rich chocolate.

Williams

Alloa, Clackmannanshire,
FK10 1NT **SCOTLAND**
www.heatherale.co.uk

Alloa was once second only
to Burton upon Trent as a
brewing center, so it is
encouraging to observe
innovative beer styles still
being developed there. Historic
recipes and traditional folklore
methods are skilfully applied.

BREWING SECRET In the Fraoch Ale,
flowering heather is used instead of hops,
reviving an ancient Celtic recipe.

Fraoch Heather Ale
SPECIALITY BITTER **4.1**% ABV
Abundantly floral and aromatic, with
a spicy mint piquancy, malty character,
and whiff of peat.

Kelpie Seaweed Ale
SPECIALITY BITTER **4.4**% ABV
Organic barley from coastal farms and
bladderwrack seaweed in the mash
produce beguiling flavors.

Wismar

Kleine Hohe Str. 15, 23966 Wismar,
GERMANY
www.brauhaus-wismar.de

In the early 15th century, there were about 180 breweries registered in Wismar, and the town was well known all over Europe. The Brauhaus Wismar was opened in 1452. Today it is the last brewery remaining in the city and, since 1995, it has brewed beer in the style of the medieval Hanseatic League breweries of northern Europe.

Wismarer Mumme

LAGER **4.8%** ABV

An old-fashioned, golden beer with lovely aromas of malt, light hops on the tongue, and a long, sweet finish.

Roter Eric

SPECIAL BEER **4.8%** ABV

The light red color comes from the malt; the beer is smooth and aromatic, with a sweet finish.

Woodforde's

Woodbastwick, Norwich, Norfolk,
NR13 6SW **ENGLAND**
www.woodfordes.co.uk

Now on its third site, the
brewery continues to increase
production capacity and to
broaden its ambitions. A
tremendous local following has
developed, and the country's top
awards have been accrued—even
for the beermats. Underpinning
all this is high-quality water,
which comes bubbling from
an on-site borehole.

Wherry Best Bitter

BEST BITTER **3.8% ABV**
Floral and citrus fruit aromas
unlock a malt-infused middle,
then a sustained finish.

Norfolk Nog

BITTER **4.6% ABV**
Deep red, with a roasted malt background
developing through liquorice nuances
and dried fruit.

Worthington's White Shield

Burton upon Trent, Staffordshire,
DE14 1YQ **ENGLAND**
www.worthingtonswhiteshield.com

The brewery, which dates from
1920, was reopened in 1995 as a
museum and in order to recreate
discontinued Bass ales, which it
has done successfully under head
brewer Steve Wellington.

BREWING SECRET White Shield became
a cult beer for aficionados, as it is bottled
"live" and improves with age.

White Shield
INDIA PALE ALE 5.6% ABV
Enthusiasts appreciate its hop attack, its
smokiness, treacle toffee sweetness,
dusting of paprika, and serving of fried
banana, stilton cheese, and sliced apple.

Yanjing

9 Shuanghe Road, Shunyi District,
Beijing, **CHINA**
www.yanjing.com.cn

The last remaining large
independent brewer in China,
Yanjing often rouses the
attention of the global brewers.
Over the past 25 years Yanjing
has developed into one of
the largest beer producing
enterprises in China. It operates
20 other breweries on the China
mainland, and its output is
predicted to reach 1.1 billion
gallons (5 million kiloliters)
by 2010.

Yanjing Beer

LAGER 5% ABV

A sweet, golden syrup nose, it has
overlays of biscuits and corn and pours
a sun burst yellow into a glass. The
brewing water is said to be from
unpolluted mineral water deep under
the Yanshan mountain.

Yoho

1119-1 Otai, Saku City,
Nagano 385-0009, **JAPAN**
www.yonasato.com

Yona Yona Ale is perhaps the
most popular craft beer in Japan,
available in brightly colored
cans and on draft all over
Japan. While the recipe predates
head brewer Toshi Ishii (who
previously worked at Stone
Brewing in San Diego), he is
responsible for their second big
success, Tokyo Black, a tasty
porter with remarkable flavor
and smooth balance.

Yona Yona Ale
PALE ALE 5.5% ABV
Square in the American Pale Ale category.
Brisk and citrussy, with Cascade hops
giving a sharp finish.

Tokyo Black
PORTER 5% ABV
This tasty, roasty beer can best be
described as a session porter, with
a unique twist. Brewer Ishii recently
brewed a batch in England.

Yukon Brewing

102A Copper Rd, Whitehorse,
Yukon Y1A 2Z6, **CANADA**
www.yukonbeer.com

Clean water makes clean beer.
Yukon beers start with North
America's cleanest water. Named
by some the Wilderness City,
Whitehorse nestles on the banks
of the famous Yukon River,
surrounded by mountains and
clear mountain lakes. Yukon
makes eight beers, including one
flavored with coffee beans.

Lead Dog Ale
ALE 7% ABV

Intricate malt flavors predominate.
Reminiscent of a porter, it has a slightly
darkened, creamy head.

Discovery Ale
PALE ALE 5% ABV

Brewed using honey made from
Fireweed, the official flower of the Yukon.
It finishes dry on the tongue.

Zagrebacka

Ilica 224, Zagreb, **CROATIA**
www.inbev.com

Zagrebacka Pivovara, Croatia's largest brewer, was established in 1893 and is now owned by InBev. After years of falling beer consumption, the market is now growing again, with domestic lager brands being the most popular segment of the market.

BREWING SECRET Double-malted dark chocolate barley gives the dark lager its prized aromas, flavors, and color.

Ožujsko Pivo
LAGER 5.2% ABV
A golden lager, with a deep, white head. A sweetcorn and malt nose gives way to a fruity finish.

Tomislav Pivo
DARK LAGER 7% ABV
Croatia's strongest beer, this deep ruby-red lager has aromas of roasted malt and coffee, and a dry finish.

Žatec

Žižkovo náměstí 81, 438 01 Žatec,
CZECH REPUBLIC
www.zateckypivovar.cz

There is no escaping it in Czech
beer production—every brewery
uses the town's succulent hops,
and, as far back as 1585, Žatec
beer was praised for "its essence,
strengths, and virtues."

BREWING SECRET Significant recent
investment has upgraded its yeast plant,
restored open fermenters, and introduced
state-of-the-art kegging.

Žatec Blue Label
PREMIUM LAGER **4.6**% ABV
Hints of grassy hop and sweet malt, then
banana with biscuit malt on the palate.

Žatec Export
PILSNER **4.6**% ABV
Bready aroma with herbal notes, some
sweet malt, delicate spicy hop, and
appropriate apple sourness.

Zlatopramen

Dráždanská 80, 400 07 Ústí nad Labem, **CZECH REPUBLIC**
www.zlatopramen.cz

Modernization may have accelerated in recent years, but this brewery's history is as long as the existence of brewing privileges. The use of Austrian Emperor Franz Joseph II's eagle for its emblem was granted in the early 20th century, while the Zlatopramen trademark was adopted in 1967. It is now owned by Drinks Union.

Zlatopramen 11°
PILSNER **4.7%** ABV
A faint, earthy hop aroma unfolds into a full biscuit flavor with a potent bitterness.

Zlatopramen 11° Dark
DARK BEER **4.6%** ABV
Aromatically floral, its sweet palate, composed from inventive blends of barley malts, edges toward toffee.

Zywiec

ul. Browarna 88, 34-300 Zywiec,
POLAND
www.zywiec.com.pl

Established in 1852 by the
Hapsburg family, this brewery
fell into state ownership after
World War II, and was acquired
by Heineken in the mid-1990s.
It is home to a lively brewing
museum that takes visitors right
through the brewing process.

BREWING SECRET The Zywiec Porter
uses a recipe from 1881.

Zywiec

LAGER 5.6% ABV
Crisp, gold, and easy-drinking, with
flowery, hoppy aromas, it is now
exported worldwide.

Porter

BALTIC PORTER 9.5% ABV
A dark, strong beer, brewed with
Munich and other special malts for
sweetness and color. Aromatic hops
provide a rich aroma.

Index

This is an index of individual beers only, as the breweries appear in A–Z order in the book.

Acknowledgments

Editor-in-Chief Tim Hampson believes he has one of the best jobs in the world—he is paid to drink beer for a living. A regular broadcaster and writer on beer for many years, he has traveled the world in pursuit of the perfect drink. Chairman of the British Guild of Beer Writers, he wants more people to understand that beer has far greater complexity than wine can ever have. And it is harder to make too. His work appears in *The Telegraph*, *Food & Travel* magazine, *What's Brewing*, *Drinks International*, *Beers of the World*, *American Brewer*, *Brewers Guardian*, and *Morning Advertiser*; he has also appeared on BBC Good Food Live and Sky TV. He is author of *Room at the Inn*.

Contributors
Tim Hampson • Stan Hieronymus • Werner Obalski • Joris Pattyn • Alastair Gilmour • Lorenzo Dabove • Gilbert Delos • Conrad Sidl • Ron Pattinson • Bryan Harrell • Willie Simpson • Geoff Griggs • Laura Stadler-Jensen • Adrian Tierney-Jones

The publishers would like to thank the following people and organizations for their help in the preparation of this book: Beers of Europe, Finn at Utobeer, Jeff at Cracked Kettle, Lithuanian Beer, Belgian Beer Shop, The Grove Tavern, Karen Heptonstall, Malini McCauley, Jennifer Crake at Tourmaline Editions, Florian Bucher, Dorothee Whittaker, Tina Gehrrig, Monika Schlitzer, Ina Melzer at DK Verlag, Dirk Kaufman at DK Inc, Rebecca Carman, Shawn Christopher, Katerina Cerna, Wojciech Kozlowski, Agnes Ordog, Jürgen Scheunemann, Yumi Shigematsu, Diggory Williams, Nora Zimerman

Images
The publishers would like to thank all the breweries that provided their kind assistance in sending bottles or bottle images to be used within this book and related works.

Thank you to the following companies for their kind permission to reproduce images for features within this book: Pelican 86 (below left); Rogue Brewery 86 (centre left)

Additional studio and location photography by Thameside Media, Quentin Bacon, Jane Ewart, Joe Giacomet, Tim Hampson, Catherine Harries, Alex Havret, Michael Jackson © DK/Michael Jackson, Roger Mapp © Rough Guides, Ian O'Leary © DK, Michael Schönwälder, Mark Thomas © Rough Guides

Maps: Casper Morris, Paul Eames, David Roberts, Iorwerth Walkins

Jacket images: (on front) Hoegaarden Wit, BridgePort India Pale Ale, Guinness Foreign Extra Stout, Starobrno Premium Lager; (on spine) U Medvídků Oldgott Barique Ležák